≻THE

CANDY
Cookbook

by
ALICE BRADLEY

Published by Hesperus Press Limited
28 Mortimer Street, London W1W 7RD
www.hesperuspress.com

The Candy Cookbook first published 1917
First published by Hesperus Press Limited, 2014

Designed and typeset by Anna Morrison
Printed in Great Britain by CPI Group (UK) Ltd, Croydon, CR0 4YY

isbn: 978-1-84391-533-1

The Candy Cookbook

By Alice Bradley

Principal of Miss Farmer's School of Cookery

Preface

Candy bought in the stores is likely to be expensive, poorly made, or impure. Candy made at home need be none of these things. And how enjoyable the process of candymaking!

What a pleasure it is some afternoon or evening when there is time to spare, to gratify the appetite with some confection, easily made! Even the little folks may take part, may help in the exciting business of manufacture, learn something of the mysteries of the kitchen, gain a little in power to use their head and hands. All of us enjoy the process and relish the product. Why, candymaking is one of those all important household pleasures that make family life mean what it does. The hours thus spent are an intimate part of that life. The writer believes, therefore, that she serves all homelovers in compiling this book. Its recipes have been thoroughly tried and tested in our school kitchens. They are simple and well adapted for ordinary use.

It is in the hope that they will be the source of many a pleasant time at home that this work is committed to its readers.

– Alice Bradley, March 1917

Contents

CHAPTER I

CANDY INGREDIENTS and Necessary Equipment

> Candies are composed of sugar of various kinds, chocolate, nuts, fruits, colorings, and flavorings. Each of these has its own particular value as appealing to the sense of sight, the sense of taste, or the need of the body for nourishment.

Sugar

Sugar ($C_{12}H_{22}O_{11}$) is a crystalline substance known by its sweet taste and its solubility in water. Sugar undergoes little change during digestion; as glucose it is carried by the blood through the body, and unites with oxygen breathed in from the air, forming carbon dioxide (CO_2), gas, and water, in which forms it leaves the body. During this change, energy is produced, and used for muscular work. Sugar is more rapidly oxidized than any other kind of foodstuff, and makes a very desirable quick fuel food.

The principal kinds of sugar are cane sugar or sucrose, grape sugar or glucose, milk sugar or lactose, and fruit sugar or levulose.

Cane sugar is obtained from sugar cane, sugar beets, and maple trees. It is sold in many forms. Granulated sugar is the kind most commonly used in candymaking. It is made by dissolving, filtering, and crystallizing the raw sugar that has been extracted from the sugar cane or sugar beet.

Brown sugar is not so completely refined as white sugar and has more flavor. Keeping it in a covered jar in a cool place prevents it from becoming lumpy.

Confectioners' sugar (icing sugar) is cane sugar so very finely ground that it is like a powder, and dissolves instantly. In recipes where it is called for other sugar cannot be substituted, although confectioners' sugar can be used in place of powdered or granulated sugar. It is a pure form of sugar with nothing added to it.

Molasses is a by-product in the manufacture of sugar, and cannot be crystallized with ordinary methods.

Maple sugar is obtained by boiling down the sap obtained by tapping maple trees. Its delicious flavor is due to 'impurities' that are present. Maple syrup can be made by dissolving maple sugar in boiling water, or by using the maple sap before it has been sufficiently reduced to become crystalline. The amount produced in this country each year is by no means sufficient to supply the demand, and consequently there are many imitations.

Grape sugar or glucose, found in honey and all sweet fruits, is less sweet than cane sugar. It may sometimes be seen on the outside of dried fruits such as dates and raisins. It is manufactured on a large scale from cornstarch, and is for sale as glucose in kegs and barrels of 110, 300 and 650 pounds each. As corn syrup or Karo, where it is combined with sugar syrup, it can be obtained in red label and blue label tins of one and one half and two and one half pounds capacity. When used in candies it prevents crystallization and gives a smoother product.

Milk sugar or lactose is present in milk, and when separated from it is sold as milk sugar. It is not sweet, and is only found in candy when milk is used.

Fruit sugar or levulose is found in sweet fruits.

It is sweeter than cane sugar and too expensive for ordinary use

Chocolate

Chocolate is obtained from cocoa beans cleaned, roasted, and finely ground. It contains much nourishment, in a concentrated form, fat, protein, and carbohydrate being present, with very little water.

Chocolate used on the outside of candies is called coating chocolate. Large candy manufacturers grind and blend cocoa beans to get the particular grade of chocolate coating for which they are famous. Sugar and vanilla are added, and any chocolate sold by name can be relied upon. It is for sale in ten-pound cakes, and should cost not less than twenty-five cents a pound for a good quality. There is upon the market a sweet coating chocolate in one sixth and half-pound cakes, in red wrappers. This can be obtained from grocers, and is very satisfactory.

Bitter or unsweetened chocolate has had nothing added to it, and should be used in fudges and other candies in which chocolate is cooked with sugar. It is for sale in quarter and half-pound cakes, divided into small squares, each weighing one ounce. Bitter chocolate is combined with sweet chocolate, and used for coating 'bitter sweets'.

Cocoa is prepared from cocoa beans by the removal of a portion of the fat. Sugar, flavorings, and sometimes starch are added.

Cocoa butter is the fat obtained from the cocoa bean in the manufacture of cocoa. A small amount is sometimes added to melted chocolate to keep it thin enough for dipping, at a moderate temperature.

Nuts

Almost all kinds of edible nuts are used in candymaking. They contain protein, fat, and carbohydrate in varying proportions, and are excellent sources of energy. Some, like peanuts and black walnuts, almonds and pine nuts, are so rich in protein that they may be used as meat substitutes. Their digestibility is increased by being finely ground. Most nuts may now be obtained shelled at about the same cost for the edible portion as in the shells. For some purposes, broken nut meats are quite satisfactory; they cost less than the whole kernels. Nuts, when used in candies, increase the bulk and food value, detract from the sweetness, and improve both appearance and flavor.

Almonds and English walnuts are the nuts chiefly grown in this country. There are both sweet and bitter almonds; the latter are used sparingly to give flavor to almond confections. Jordan almonds are the finest almonds grown, and are for sale out of the shell, as are also other smaller and shorter varieties.

Almond paste may be made at home of finely ground almonds, but it is more satisfactory to purchase it ready for use in one and five-pound packages.

Brazil nuts are large three-cornered nuts, with a hard shell and a brown skin. The latter should usually be removed before the nuts are used in candy. Beechnuts and butternuts (white walnuts) are not often found in the market, but if obtainable may be used in recipes that call for walnuts or pecans.

Cashew nuts are small crescent-shaped nuts, and are usually sold with the shells removed.

Chestnuts should be of the large Spanish variety. They are rich in starch, and when boiled in syrup are a delicious confection. They may be purchased in bottles as 'marrons' in vanilla or brandy-flavored syrup, and used for centers of fancy bonbons, chocolates, or glacés.

Coconut may be purchased desiccated in packages, or as 'desiccated', 'long', 'short', or 'macaroon', in bulk from wholesale confectioners. The very long shreds of coconut are desirable in some candies. Fresh-grated coconut should be used for coconut cakes if obtainable.

Coconut oil is a very hard fat, for sale as nucoa and used in chewing-candy.

Hazelnuts are round, about the size of a marble, and rich in fat. They are usually purchased in the shell.

Hickory nuts are like small walnuts, but the meat is difficult to remove whole from the shell, although delicious when obtained.

Peanuts are grown in larger and larger quantities in the United States, and furnish a nutritious and inexpensive food product, rich in protein and fat. They may be obtained raw or roasted, in or out of the shell. Raw peanuts are desirable in some recipes for peanut brittle.

Peanut butter is made by putting roasted peanuts through the finest cutter of the meat grinder, and may be prepared at home, or purchased in jars or in bulk by the pound.

Pecans are a particularly crisp, well-flavored nut. If they are first soaked for 5 hours in cold water, and then allowed to stand until dried off on the outside, the nut meats can be obtained whole. They may be purchased shelled, whole, or broken.

Pine nuts grow on pine cones of large pine trees. They have an agreeable flavor, are rich in fat and of considerable food value. They require no other preparation than picking over.

Pistachio nuts are small, of a bright green color, with a purplish skin and a hard shell. The unshelled nuts have been boiled in salt water. They usually are not of such brilliant color as the nuts that may be purchased already shelled. They are expensive but not heavy, and a few of them add much to the attractiveness of candies without adding materially to the expense. They will keep a long time in a covered glass jar.

Walnuts of the English variety are obtainable almost everywhere. Being rich in fats they are an exceedingly nutritious food, and when used in candies help to overcome the cloying sweetness while increasing the food value. They may be obtained in or out of the shell.

Black walnuts are not as common as the English varieties but most satisfactory in all candies that call for walnuts.

Dairy Products

Milk, cream, and butter enter into the composition of many candies. Heavy cream makes a rich candy that will keep soft for a long time, and may be used either sweet or sour. When cream is not available milk and butter may be substituted, or evaporated milk may be used.

Butter should be of the best quality. Butterine or peanut oil is less expensive, and may sometimes be substituted for butter.

Eggs

Eggs for candy should be fresh. If whites only are required, care should be taken in separating that no particle of yolk gets into the white, as it will prevent its being beaten light and stiff. Bowl and egg beater must be absolutely clean, dry, and cool, or whites will not beat up well. Dried eggs or egg albumen are largely used in manufactured candies.

Fruits

Fresh, canned, and dried fruits are used in candy-making, and add bulk and flavor, while reducing the sweetness. Fresh fruits may be dipped in fondant, chocolate, or glacé, or cooked down to a thick jelly.

Canned fruits, as apricots or pineapple, are useful when fresh fruits are not obtainable, and jams, like raspberry, may be mixed with fondant for bonbon centers. Maraschino cherries are sometimes used, with their syrup, to give flavor and variety to fudge and bonbons.

Dried fruits, like raisins, dates, figs, and prunes, are cheap and nutritious. Combined with nuts or fondant they may be classed with candies and used as a dessert.

Candied fruits – such as apricots, cherries, pears, pineapple, and plums – may be prepared at home, or purchased in city grocery stores, or from dealers in confectioners' supplies. They are valuable for decoration, for centers of chocolates and bonbons, and as an ingredient of fudges and glacéd fruits.

Angelica is the green stem of a plant, used chiefly for its color.

Flavorings

Extract of vanilla properly made is the pure essence of the vanilla bean dissolved in alcohol.

Many vanilla extracts are made from Tonka beans, or from vanillin prepared synthetically in a laboratory. These are labeled vanilla compounds.

Extracts of lemon and orange are made by dissolving in alcohol, oil obtained from the yellow skin of the fruit.

Raspberry, strawberry, cherry, apple, pineapple, banana, and other familiar fruit flavors constitute a class of flavoring extracts similar in character and similarly made.

Attar or otto of rose, one of the first perfumes and perhaps the most exquisite of all, is the base of true rose extract.

Ginger extract is made by steeping and filtering ground ginger roots in alcohol.

Almond oil is procured by pressing, powdering, and drying bitter almonds, allowing the mixture to ferment, and then distilling it by steam. Almond extract is the oil dissolved in alcohol.

Pistachio flavor can better be simulated in candy by using one part almond extract and two parts vanilla extract than by using pistachio extract.

Peppermint oil is distilled from dried peppermint plants.

Maple flavor is a preparation of roots and herbs used to give a maple taste to white or brown sugar candy.

All spice extracts are made either by dissolving an essential oil in alcohol or percolating a ground bark with alcohol.

Colorings

The varied color of candies may be due to the food materials of which they are made, or to small amounts of coloring matter added to them. Satisfactory pastes may be obtained in eight colors, in small glass jars selling for fifteen or twenty-five cents each. They are inspected and registered by the United States Government. Small amounts only are required for the delicate shades that are desirable in first-class candies. The color may be taken on the end of a toothpick and mixed directly with the candy, or be diluted with a few drops of water before being added.

Gelatine

Gelatine is obtained by the treatment of skin, ligaments, and bones of young calves with boiling water. It is for sale in sheets, in shreds, or granulated. The latter is most convenient to use, but sheet gelatine is considered best for Turkish paste.

Vegetable Gelatine

Agar-agar, or Japanese gelatine, is used by many candy manufacturers, and is for sale at confectioners' supply houses.

Marshmallow Paste

Marshmallows which are made by strong beating machinery are cheaper and more satisfactory than those made at home. For use in layer caramels, marshmallow comes in sheets weighing one pound each. There are five sheets in a box. The soft marshmallow cream that is sold in tin boxes may be added to fudge to make it soft and creamy.

Food Value of Candy

Food is required to furnish energy and heat to the body, and material for growth, repair, and for the regulation of body processes.

Heat and energy are estimated in calories, the average person requiring enough food in the form of fat, starch, sugar, and protein, to furnish about 2,500 calories a day.

Material for growth and repair is furnished by protein foods, of which from sixty to one hundred grams per day are needed, and by water and various ash constituents which are also needed to maintain the body in health.

Candy, especially when it contains fruit and nuts, can supply both calories and protein, and is therefore to be reckoned as food. Large amounts of candy taken in addition to regular meals may lead to increase in body weight, and to serious digestive disturbance. Reasonable amounts may well take the place of other desserts, or may be used to furnish energy in an emergency, as on a long tramp.

Recipes

For satisfactory results in candymaking, as in other kinds of cooking with tested recipes, accurate measurements are necessary. With half-pint measuring cups divided into quarters and thirds, with teaspoons, tablespoons, and a case knife, the ingredients in the following recipes can be put together without the use of scales.

The table at the end of this book can be used to determine how much of any material needs to be purchased, or to change cup measurements to pounds or ounces.

Most of the recipes in this book are proportioned to make one pound of candy.

How To Measure

To measure a cup of dry material like sugar, fill the cup by putting in the sugar with a scoop or large spoon, until cup overflows, and level off with a knife. Tablespoons and teaspoons are filled and leveled in the same way. Divide with knife lengthwise of spoon for a half-spoonful; divide halves crosswise for quarters, and quarters crosswise for eighths. A cupful or spoonful of liquid is all the cup or spoon will hold. Less than a cupful of material should be measured to the proper mark upon the cup. Less than one eighth of a teaspoon is called a few grains.

Equipment for Home Candymaking

Many varieties of candy can be made without any other utensils than are found in the average kitchen. The following list will be sufficient for the preparation of any candies found in this book. When candy is to be made commercially on a large scale, many other pieces of equipment will be found desirable.

List of Utensils Desirable in Candymaking

Saucepan, 1 pint, agate or aluminum
Saucepan, 1 quart, agate or aluminum
Saucepan, 3 pint, agate or aluminum
Double boiler, 1 quart
Cup, half-pint, agate
Scotch kettle, iron or copper
Frying pan, iron

Case knife, 6 inches long
Spatula, 8 inches long
Wide spatula, 2½ inches wide, 6 inches long
Two-tined fork
Butter brush, rubber set
Wire bonbon dippers
Small round cutters
Small fancy cutters
Tin grater
Bowls, agate or crockery
Purée sieve
Wire strainer
Rolling pin
Marble slab or white agate tray
Cake pans
Scales
Wire whisks
Egg beaters
Half-pint measuring cups divided in quarters
Half-pint measuring cups divided in thirds
Teaspoons
Tablespoons
Wooden spoon, long handle
Mixing spoon, long handle
Sharp knife, 8 inches long
Sharp knife, 4 inches long
Candy thermometer
Small pair tweezers
Candy hook, to be attached to the wall
Plaster of Paris molds
Tin confectioners' funnel for dropping candies
Steel bars
Sugar spinner
Nut cracker
Food chopper
White table oilcloth
Wax paper
Rice paper

Chocolate dipping paper
Paper cases
Cheesecloth
Timbale irons
Covered jars
Pastry bag and tubes

Saucepans and double boilers may be of agateware or aluminum. Tin is not desirable. An agate cup is useful for melting butter with which to grease pans.

An iron frying pan, or copper or iron Scotch kettle, is best for candies that are cooked to a very high temperature.

A marble slab is most convenient for receiving hot candies that are later worked with a spatula until creamy. A white agate tray, like those used by butchers for displaying meat, or a large platter, may be substituted. For turning over and scraping up the candy nothing is better than a wide, flexible steel spatula. A wooden butter paddle may be used, but it is not as convenient.

Bonbon dippers may be purchased or fashioned at home from a piece of Number 14 wire. They should be six inches long and the open bowl of dipper three quarters of an inch across.

Steel or iron bars, sixteen inches long and three quarters of an inch square, are convenient to keep the candy from running off a marble slab. The opening between may be made of any size, and candy may thus be cooled on the marble without the use of a pan.

Sugar spinners are made of a bundle of twenty coarse wires, ten inches long, fastened together at one end with wire coiled round and round to make a handle. A large wire egg whip, with the wires cut at the end, answers the purpose perfectly.

Paraffin or wax paper comes in different weights. The thinnest paper is generally used for wrapping caramels, or for receiving dipped candies. Chocolate dipping paper is stiff, with a high gloss on one side, and is desirable for receiving dipped chocolates, although white table oilcloth is equally good, and may be used over and over again. Rice paper is used for the top and bottom of nougatines, and may be eaten with the candy.

Candy Thermometer

For accurate and uniform results in candymaking, a thermometer that registers up to 400°F (204.4°C) is almost indispensable.

Much experience is necessary to determine correctly the required condition by testing candy in cold water. With careful usage, a thermometer should last for years. It may be obtained at hardware and kitchen furnishing stores for one dollar and upwards.

Care of Thermometer

The thermometer should be placed in syrup before the boiling point is reached, in order to avoid heating it too suddenly. If it is necessary to put it into candy heated beyond the boiling point, it should be held for a few moments just above the liquid that it may become warm, and then lowered gradually into syrup. When removing thermometer from candy, place it immediately in boiling water or very hot water, and allow it to cool slowly.

The following table gives tests for sugar syrup and corresponding degree on the thermometer.

Crystal syrup	220°F (104.4°C)
Soft ball	238°F (114.4°C)
Medium ball	240°F (115.5°C)
Stiff ball	244°F (117.7°C)
Hard ball	250°F (121.1°C)
Light crack	264°F (128.9°C)
Medium crack	272°F (133.3°C)
Hard crack	290°F (143.3°C)
Extra hard crack	330°F (165.5°C)
Caramel	360°F (182.2°C)

CHAPTER II

UNCOOKED Candies

For inexperienced candymakers, and the children who want to make their own sweets, there are several varieties of uncooked candy that can hardly fail to come out successfully.

Confectioners' sugar (icing sugar) must be used where called for, or the candies will not harden properly. This sugar should be kept in a closely covered jar or pail and be sifted before using, to free it from lumps. If the lumps are very hard, a large sheet of clean paper should be spread on the table and the sugar rolled on it with a rolling pin until smooth, then sifted through a fine sieve.

Uncooked Cream Fondant

2 tbsp heavy cream
1 cup confectioners' sugar (icing sugar)
1 teaspoon corn syrup
Flavors
Colors

Put cream and light-colored corn syrup in a bowl, add sifted sugar gradually, stirring until smooth, and add as much sugar as is necessary to make a stiff paste. Add flavoring or coloring as desired and use as a filling for dates, fruits, nuts, or as centers for bonbons or chocolates.

It may be warmed (but not made hot) over hot water, and nuts, cherries, grapes, sections of orange, and fondant centers be dipped in it. It will have to be kept over the hot water, stirred constantly, and frequently put for a few moments over the fire. See directions for dipping on page 33.

Uncooked Egg Fondant

1 egg white
½ tsp vanilla
1 tbsp cold water
2 cups confectioners' sugar (icing sugar)

Put egg white, water, and flavoring in a bowl, and beat until well blended. Sift sugar and add one spoonful at a time, stirring until well mixed, before each addition.

Continue adding a spoonful at a time until mixture is very stiff, then take out on a board, and knead with the hands until perfectly smooth. Use as stuffing for dates, for nut creams, or for centers for chocolates and bonbons.

Fondant may be colored by the addition of pink, green, yellow, lavender, or orange color paste, and other flavors may be used instead of vanilla.

Almond Creams

Almonds
Fondant
Plain or colored granulated sugar

Blanch almonds (see page 148), and place one on each side of a small ball of fondant, or cover almonds with fondant, shape like a very small egg, and roll in granulated sugar.

Cherry Creams I

Fondant
Candied cherries

Take fondant, cooked or uncooked, of any color or flavour, roll out one eighth inch thick, shape with round cutter one and one half inches in diameter, and roll around cherry, leaving a small portion exposed. Place in paper cases. Vanilla, coffee, and pistachio fondant look particularly well with the cherries.

Cherry Creams II

Select as many firm, smooth, candied cherries as are desired. Cut each cherry, starting at the open end, into four sections, and separate into petals. Make a tiny hole at the other end, and insert a strip of angelica one and one half inches long for a stem. Place a small ball of fondant between the petals, and arrange on a doily, or use on top of a box of bonbons.

Cherry Creams III

Cut candied cherries almost in two; between the halves of each cherry place a flat ball of fondant, press together gently, and roll in coarse granulated sugar.

Uncooked Coconut Creams

3 tbsp heavy cream
½ tsp violet essence or vanilla
Lavender color paste
1 cup confectioners' sugar (icing sugar)
1 cup shredded coconut

Color the heavy cream a deep shade of lavender, add flavoring and coconut, and let stand 10 minutes. Then add sifted sugar, heat over hot water until softened, and drop from the tip of a fork on wax paper, in rough balls the size of a chocolate cream. Leave until firm. Color paste may be omitted, or other colors may be used instead of lavender.

Coffee Creams

4 tbsp water
2 tbsp ground coffee
1½ cups confectioners' sugar (icing sugar)

Put water and coffee in a saucepan, bring to the boiling point, boil 2 minutes, and strain through double cheesecloth. Add sufficient confectioners' sugar to stiffen, and knead until smooth. Use for walnut, pecan, or cherry creams, as centers for chocolates or bonbons, or roll out one fourth inch thick, cut with a small round cutter, and roll in granulated sugar.

Date Creams

Dates
Fondant
Chopped nuts

Wash dates and remove stones. Fondant, either cooked or uncooked, may be used. Flavor and color fondant as desired, roll in small cylinders, put into the dates where the stone was removed, and roll in granulated sugar. Pile on a bonbon dish, or pack in layers in a candy box with waxed paper between each layer. Chopped nuts may be mixed with the fondant, or the edge of the fondant projecting from the date may be dipped in chopped nuts.

Uncooked Fudge

7 oz sweet coating chocolate
2 eggs
1 cup English walnut meats
1 tbsp butter
1 cup confectioners' sugar (icing sugar)
1½ tsp vanilla

Melt chocolate over hot water, add butter, sugar, yolks of eggs beaten until thick and lemon colored, whites of eggs beaten stiff, walnuts cut in pieces, and vanilla. Spread in buttered pan, and when firm cut in squares. This fudge is always soft and creamy.

Ginger Creams

2 tbsp ginger syrup
4 tbsp chopped preserved ginger
Confectioners' sugar (icing sugar)

Mix syrup from a jar of preserved ginger with two tablespoons of the chopped ginger, and add sifted confectioners' sugar until stiff enough to knead. Knead until smooth, shape in small balls, and decorate with small pieces of preserved ginger.

Lemon Creams

2 tbsp lemon juice
Few drops lemon extract
Sifted confectioners' sugar (icing sugar)
Yellow color paste

Mix lemon juice and extract, and add sugar slowly until stiff enough to knead, adding color paste to make a delicate yellow. Knead with the hands until smooth, roll one fourth inch thick, and cut out with a small round cutter.

Maple Nut Creams

4 tbsp maple syrup
1 cup confectioners' sugar (icing sugar)
6 tbsp chopped nuts

Put maple syrup in a small bowl, add sifted confectioners' sugar a tablespoon at a time, stirring until smooth, and adding sufficient sugar to make candy stiff. Knead until smooth. Shape in small balls, and roll in nut meats.

Frosted Nuts

1 tsp corn syrup
Few drops maraschino or vanilla
2 tbsp boiling water
Confectioners' sugar (icing sugar)

Put corn syrup, boiling water, and one fourth cup sifted confectioners' sugar in a saucepan or bowl, and stir until ingredients are thoroughly mixed. Then add another quarter cup of sugar, and beat vigorously until thick and smooth. Continue adding sugar, one fourth cup at a time, and beating between each addition of sugar, until about two cups of sugar have been used. Flavor with maraschino cordial or vanilla. This frosting should be kept at an even, lukewarm temperature while it is being made, and the saucepan or bowl should be frequently placed in a larger bowl of hot water. The beating of this frosting should continue for about 20 minutes.

Dip walnuts, hazelnuts, Brazil nuts, or hickory nuts, one at a time, into the frosting, and remove with a fork or candy dipper to an oiled marble slab or to waxed paper.

Orange Cream

Grated rind ½ orange
1 tsp lemon juice
1 tsp orange juice
1 egg yolk
2 cups sifted confectioners' sugar (icing sugar)

Before cutting the orange, wipe carefully, and grate the yellow part only from the skin; then cut the orange in two and extract the juice.

Mix rind and fruit juice, let stand 10 minutes, and strain. Add slowly to the egg yolk, and when well mixed add sugar gradually until stiff enough to knead. Knead until smooth, and use for date, nut, prune, or cherry creams, or for centers of chocolates or bonbons.

Prune Creams

Large prunes
Orange juice
Orange fondant or orange cream
Granulated sugar

Wash prunes, soak until plump in orange juice to cover, then steam until soft. Drain, remove stones, fill prunes with fondant rolled into balls a little larger than a prune stone, close the prunes, and roll in granulated sugar.

Decorated Peppermints

1 egg white
2 drops oil of peppermint
½ tbsp cold water
Confectioners' sugar (icing sugar)

Put white of egg, cold water, and peppermint in a bowl, beat until very light, and add sugar a tablespoon at a time, beating between each addition, until mixture is stiff enough to hold its shape. Reserve one third of the mixture, and add sugar slowly to the remainder until it is stiff enough to knead. Work it with the hands until smooth, put on a board, roll out one eighth inch thick, and cut with a small round cutter. Decorate with the remaining mixture, colored pink, blue, lavender, yellow, or green, forced through paper tubes, making tiny roses, forget-me-nots, violets, or sweet peas, with stems and leaves on each mint, as described in Chapter XV.

Children will amuse themselves for hours making original designs with different colored frostings, and will exhibit their results with the greatest pride at the close of the happy afternoon. Half a dozen paper cones may be provided as described on page 177, and filled with different colored frostings. If color pastes are not at hand, a bit of melted chocolate may be used in one portion, the yolk of an egg in another; a color tablet from a box of gelatine, dissolved in a few drops of water, will answer very well to color a third portion.

Potato Coconut Candy

1 medium sized potato
2 cups shredded coconut
2 cups sifted confectioners' sugar (icing sugar)
1 tsp vanilla
Chocolate

Cook potato in boiling water until soft, and force through a coarse sieve or a potato ricer.

There should be half a cup of potato. To this add sugar, coconut, and vanilla, working together until well mixed. Press one inch thick into small bread pan, and spread top with a thin layer of melted bitter chocolate or sweet chocolate. When chocolate is firm, cut in small squares. This can be varied by using nuts or fruits instead of coconut.

Uncooked Strawberry Creams

½ cup strawberries
Sifted confectioners' sugar (icing sugar)
½ tsp lemon juice

Wash and hull strawberries, sprinkle with half a cup of confectioners' sugar, and let stand half an hour. Mash, rub through a fine sieve, add lemon juice, and stir in, a tablespoon at a time, enough more confectioners' sugar to make mixture stiff enough to shape. Make into small balls, and roll in granulated sugar, or roll out in a sheet one fourth inch thick, cut with small round cutter, and roll in sugar, or dip in melted coating chocolate.

Other fruit, or syrup from a well-flavored jar of fruit, may be used instead of strawberries.

Walnut Creams

Fondant
English walnut meats

Use any of the recipes for cooked or uncooked fondant, color and flavor as desired, shape in small balls, using one tablespoon of fondant for each ball. Press half of a walnut meat firmly on each side, and roll edges in granulated sugar, either plain or colored.

Maple, vanilla, or coffee flavor are good, or raspberry flavor and pink color paste may be used.

Pecan Creams

Follow recipe for Walnut Creams, using pecan nut meats in place of walnuts.

More than a hundred different chocolates may be found in the price lists of some manufacturers. Almost all of them may be duplicated at home, if care is taken to follow directions explicitly. Regular coating chocolate must be used for dipping. It may be bitter chocolate, sweet chocolate, milk chocolate, or what is known as bittersweet chocolate coating, and is obtainable in ten-pound cakes. These will be sold in pieces of smaller size by dealers in confectioners' supplies. During the melting and use of the chocolate the greatest care must be taken that the temperature is right. Full directions will be found farther on in this chapter. Before preparing the chocolate the centers must be made ready.

Centers for Chocolates

Chocolate creams may have centers that are hard or soft, and of many different flavors, colors, and shapes. Fondant either cooked or uncooked, made by recipes in Chapters II and III, may be used. Directions for making centers are found on page 82. They should be small, as the chocolate coating adds to their original size.

Caramels should be cut smaller than when used without coating, as should fudge, nougatines, marshmallows, candied fruits, or fruit pastes. Nuts should be shelled, and sometimes blanched, and be perfectly dry. Dragées and other decorations for the tops of the candies should be ready for immediate use. Several kinds of centers may be made ready at one time, and then dipped one after another. A pound box can be soon filled with assorted chocolates.

The name of the center gives the name to the chocolate; thus almonds dipped in melted chocolate are called chocolate almonds; almonds dipped in fondant and then in chocolate are chocolate cream almonds. The following suggestions for centers for assorted chocolates may be extended almost indefinitely.

Almonds
Almonds blanched and dipped in white fondant
Almond paste shaped in balls, or cut in strips or cubes
Apricot paste in cubes or fancy shapes

Brazil nuts, shelled
Brazil nuts, brown skin removed, mixed with chocolate opera fudge
Butterscotch wafers
Butterscotch wafers, with peanuts

Center cream, with and without nuts, and variously colored and
flavored
Checkerberries, dipped in fondant

Cherries, candied, dipped in fondant
Chocolate caramels
Chocolate fudge with walnuts
Coconut, shredded
Coconut caramels
Coffee beans, freshly roasted
Coffee fondant

Dates, stuffed with salted peanuts or peanut butter
Dates stuffed with opera fondant

Fig caramels
Fig creams

Hazelnut, dropped three together, in a row, or clover leaf shape

Fondant, flavored and colored as suggested on page 84, and mixed
with nuts, candied fruits, or jam
Fruit cake

Ginger, preserved, mixed with opera fondant, bit of ginger on top of
chocolate
Grapefruit peel, candied

Maple cream
Maple cream with walnuts
Maple cream with blanched almond or walnut on top of each chocolate
Maraschino cherries dipped in fondant
Marshmallow caramels
Marshmallows
Mint jelly
Nabisco wafers cut in pieces
Nougatines

Opera fudge, all flavors
Orange peel, candied
Oyster crackers

Peanuts, roasted, dropped in bunches of three or four
Peanut brittle
Peanut butter cream
Peanut butter fudge
Pecan nut meats, whole
Pecans dipped in coffee fondant
Pecans dipped in maple cream, whole pecan on top
Peppermints

Pineapple, dried canned fruit, or candied pineapple, dipped in cherry-flavored fondant
Bit of pineapple on top of chocolate

Raisins, large, seeded, dipped in fondant or stuffed with fondant flavored with vanilla
Raspberry jam mixed with opera fondant, bit of candied rose petal on top

Turkish delight

Vanilla caramels

Walnut meats whole
Walnut meats dipped in maple cream, whole walnut on top
Wedding cake

The centers should be kept in the room in which they are to be used, that they may be neither too warm nor too cold. When a sufficient supply of centers is ready, the chocolate may be prepared.

To Melt Chocolate

Sweetened, unsweetened, or milk coating chocolate should be used (see page 9), and it is not wise to start with less than one pound. More than that is desirable even for a small amount of candy, as it keeps at the right consistency for dipping for a longer time, and that which is not used at once can be melted and used later. Some authorities say that never less than five pounds should be melted at one time.

The room in which the dipping is to be done should be free from steam and of an even temperature of about 65° to 75°F (18°C to 24°C). On a hot or a rainy day, chocolate dipping should not be attempted at home.

Break chocolate in pieces, and put into a double boiler or saucepan over hot water. The two pans should fit closely, that the steam may not escape. Set both pans over the fire until water boils in the lower pan. Remove from fire, and stir until chocolate is melted, then remove dish from hot water to ice water, and beat chocolate gently until it feels a little cooler than the hand, or registers between 80°F and 85° F (25°C and 30°C) on the thermometer.

To Dip Chocolates

When large numbers of centers are to be dipped, the melted chocolate is poured on a marble slab, and the beating is done with the hand and the dipping with the fingers. Much experience is necessary to produce the markings seen on the best chocolates. The amateur will probably prefer to use a wire bonbon dipper or a two-tined fork. For small centers, like nuts, a small pair of tweezers is useful.

Set the dish of chocolate on the table with centers to be dipped on the left, and chocolate dipping paper, paraffin paper, or white table oilcloth on the right. It is well to have the paper on small boards or tin sheets that candies may be easily moved.

Drop a center into melted chocolate; with the dipper move it around until covered, then lift out, upside down, scrape off superfluous chocolate on the edge of the pan, and place bonbon on the paper right side up. Make a line of chocolate over the top of the bonbon when removing the dipper. Different designs on top sometimes indicate the kind of center. Between the dipping of every bonbon the chocolate must be thoroughly beaten.

Chocolates sometimes harden very quickly. On a warm day they must be put in the refrigerator as soon as coated, for 10 minutes or until hard.

If the chocolate is neither too warm nor too cool and was beaten sufficiently, and chocolates were cooled quickly enough, they will have a gloss and retain the markings perfectly. If they are gray or streaked, they did not cool quickly enough. If spotted, the chocolate was not beaten enough. If chocolate runs off and forms a thick base, it was not cool enough. If the least bit of steam or water gets in it, the chocolate will become thick and unfit for coating but may be used for cooking purposes. If it does not remain thin enough for dipping, a small piece of cocoa butter may be added, or the water underneath may be heated slightly, when chocolate must be beaten again. Chocolate may be left in the dish in which it was melted and be ready for use at any time.

Decorating Chocolates

If chocolates are to be decorated, the nut, dragées, candied fruit, or other decoration must be put in place as soon as the bonbon is placed on the paper. Chocolates may be rolled in coconut, chopped roasted almonds, or pistachio nuts immediately after dipping. Chopped nuts may be stirred into the melted chocolate before the centers are dipped.

Do not remove dipped chocolates from wax paper or oilcloth until the bottom is glossy and chocolate is firm.

Keeping Chocolates

Chocolates should be packed in boxes between layers of wax paper as soon as hard. A few of the chocolates may be wrapped in gold or silver foil. They should be kept in a cool, dry place, and should at no time be exposed to the rays of the sun. They should not be placed in the vicinity of articles that give off strong odors, as chocolate is very absorbent.

Solid Chocolate Shapes

Prepare coating chocolate as for dipping and beat until cool enough to hold its shape. Put into a cloth or paper pastry bag with a small tin rose tube in the end. Force chocolate upon chocolate dipping paper, paraffin paper, or table oilcloth in small fancy shapes, as roses, spirals, or bars, and leave until firm. Some of the pieces may be sprinkled with a very little coarse granulated sugar, flavored with peppermint, and colored pink or green. Milk coating chocolate is particularly good in this way.

Green Mint Sugar

1 cup sugar
2 drops green color paste
1 drop oil of peppermint

Put sugar in a small bowl, add a drop of oil of peppermint, then, using a spoon, work in the green color paste, a tiny bit at a time, until the desired shade is obtained. Pink color paste and oil of wintergreen may be substituted for green color paste and oil of peppermint. Other colors, with or without flavor, may be substituted for either.

Almond Tulips

Fondant blanched almonds
Coating chocolate
Almond extract

Flavor fondant with almond extract, and make into balls, shaping them high and pointed. Dip in melted coating chocolate, and put three halved blanched almonds on the sides.

Burnt Almond Chocolates I

Cover almonds with boiling water, let stand 2 minutes, cover with cold water, drain and remove brown skins. Put in pan, and leave in moderate oven until a golden brown. Cool and dip in melted coating chocolate.

Burnt Almond Chocolates II

Fondant blanched almonds
½ cup almonds
½ cup fondant
Coating chocolate

Prepare almonds as in previous recipe. When golden brown, cut in pieces, mix with fondant, shape in balls, let dry on wax paper, and dip in melted coating chocolate.

Roast Almond Chocolates

Coarsely chop roasted almonds, mix with melted milk chocolate to make a thick paste, and drop with a spoon in small pieces on wax paper.

Bittersweet Chocolate Creams

Center Cream II (see p. 80)
1 lb sweet coating chocolate
½ lb bitter chocolate late
1 tsp vanilla

Make center cream as given on page 80, and shape in small balls. Put both kinds of chocolate in upper part of double boiler, and prepare for dipping as explained in the first part of this chapter. Just before beginning to dip, add vanilla and beat thoroughly. Dip centers one at a time, and remove to wax paper. Use coating as cold as possible in order to retain the gloss.

Chocolate Butterscotch Creams

Make Cream Butterscotch Balls (see page 115), and leave mixture in the buttered pan. Cover with melted fondant flavored with vanilla, and when firm cut in small pieces, and dip in melted coating chocolate.

Chocolate Coffee Beans

Coating chocolate
Fresh roasted coffee beans

Melt chocolate over hot water, being careful that not a drop of water gets into the chocolate; then beat it until cool. Dip freshly roasted coffee beans in the chocolate; lift out with a fork, and drop on wax paper or marble slab to harden. Blanched almonds or Brazil nuts, hazelnuts, peanuts, pecans, or walnuts may be coated in the same way.

Coconut Chocolate Ruffs

¼ lb coating chocolate
1½ cups coconut

Melt chocolate over hot water, and stir in all the long strip coconut it will coat and hold. Take out pieces the size of a marble, and lay on wax paper to dry. This is an excellent way to utilize a small amount of chocolate that may be left from dipping centers.

Chocolate Fig Creams

6 figs
Confectioners' sugar (icing sugar)

Chop figs finely, and slowly add sifted confectioners' sugar until mixture is stiff enough to mold into small balls. Shape, let dry, and dip in melted coating chocolate.

Chocolate Fig Paste

¼ lb figs
¾ cup fondant
Sweet coating chocolate

Put figs through meat chopper, and mix with fondant, kneading together until perfectly smooth. Shape in small balls, and dip in melted coating chocolate.

Jelly Chocolates

1 cup apple jelly
¼ cup cold water
2 tbsp gelatine
1 tsp orange extract
½ tsp lemon extract

Melt apple jelly over hot water, add gelatine soaked in cold water, and extracts. Strain into small molds or into a bread pan half an inch thick. When firm, remove from molds, and if in a sheet, cut the jelly in cubes. Dip in melted coating chocolate.

Nut Fritters

Mix broken pecan nut meats, roasted Spanish peanuts, or roasted almonds, with just enough cool chocolate to hold them together. Drop from tip of spoon in rough piles as large as a half dollar.

Chocolate Maraschino Cherries

Maraschino cherries
Fondant
Coating chocolate

Drain as many cherries as are wanted, and dip them in melted fondant. When all are covered, dip into melted coating chocolate. If a drop of syrup breaks through the chocolate, cover the spot with melted chocolate. The fondant will very soon liquefy in the center.

Chocolate Liquor Drops

2 cups sugar
Few grains cream of tartar
1 cup water
2 tbsp maraschino cordial

Boil sugar, water, and cream of tartar to 235° F (112.7°C). Add maraschino cordial, and boil up once. Cool for 2 minutes. Pour into starch molds, cover with starch, let stand 24 hours, brush off starch, and dip in melted coating chocolate, or crystallize.

Chocolate Chestnuts

⅓ cup preserved chestnuts
1 cup fondant
Coating chocolate

Break the preserved chestnuts in two or three pieces, and dip in melted fondant; or crush preserved chestnuts, mix with fondant, and shape in small balls. When firm, dip in melted coating chocolate.

Chocolate Marshmallows I

Cut marshmallows across, and stuff with a pecan nut meat or a piece of Canton ginger. Press together and dip in melted coating chocolate.

Chocolate Marshmallows II

Marshmallows
Melted coating chocolate
Chopped blanched almonds

Mix almonds with twice the amount of melted coating chocolate, and when beaten until cool, dip marshmallows, one at a time, and drop on wax paper.

Chocolate-dipped Candied Orange Peel

Prepare Candied Orange Peel (see page 131), dip each orange straw separately in melted coating chocolate, and lay on wax paper to dry.

Chocolate-dipped Candied Grapefruit Peel

Prepare Candied Grapefruit Peel (see page 131), dip each grapefruit straw separately in melted coating chocolate, and lay on wax paper to dry.

Chocolate Peanut Butter Creams

½ cup fondant
½ tsp vanilla
3 tbsp peanut butter
Few grains salt
Coating chocolate

Mix fondant, peanut butter, salt, and vanilla with a spatula on marble slab or plate until thoroughly blended. Shape in small balls, and dip in melted coating chocolate. Mix fondant, peanut butter, salt, and vanilla with a spatula on marble slab or plate until thoroughly blended. Shape in small balls, and dip in melted coating chocolate.

Chocolate Peppermints I

Fondant
Oil of peppermint
Coating chocolate

Melt fondant over hot water, flavor to taste with one or more drops of oil of peppermint, and drop from tip of spoon on waxed paper, or into starch impressions (see page 82) the size and shape of peppermints. When firm, dip in melted coating chocolate.

Chocolate Peppermints II

2 tbsp hot top milk
½ tsp melted butter
2 cups confectioners' sugar (icing sugar)
3 drops oil of peppermint

Mix hot milk, one and one half cups sifted confectioners' sugar, butter, and peppermint, add more sugar as needed to make stiff, and then knead on a marble slab or a board for 10 minutes, or until candy is creamy in texture. Shape with the hands into balls, or roll out on a board, and cut with small round cutter, and dip in melted coating chocolate.

Pine Nut Chocolates

½ cup pine nuts
Few grains salt
½ cup fondant
Melted coating chocolate
1 tbsp almond paste
Chopped pine nuts

Place half a cup of pine nuts in oven, and bake until a delicate brown. Chop fine, mix evenly with fondant, almond paste, and salt, shape in small balls, dip in melted coating chocolate, and roll at once in unroasted chopped pine nuts.

Other nuts may be substituted for the pine nuts.

Three-in-One Chocolates

Hazelnuts
Fondant
Candied cherries Vanilla
Coating chocolate

Cover hazelnuts with boiling water and leave 2 minutes. Drain, cover with cold water, remove skins, and dry on a towel. Flavor fondant with vanilla, and shape in balls the size of the nuts. Dip first a nut, then a cherry, then a ball of fondant in melted coating chocolate, place close together on oilcloth or wax paper, and join with a line of chocolate.

Chocolate Truffles

Fondant or center cream
Milk chocolate
Shredded coconut

Make very small centers from any of the recipes for fondant or center cream in Chapter V, dip in melted milk chocolate, then roll at once in shredded coconut, chopped fine.

Chocolate Washington Pies

Fondant
Coating chocolate
Raspberry or strawberry jam

Put a piece of firm fondant on a marble slab or bread board, roll out one fourth inch thick, cover half of it with stiff raspberry or strawberry jam; on top place remaining layer of fondant, and cut out with small round cutter. Leave until dry, and dip in melted chocolate.

The trimmings may be gathered up, and worked together into little balls which may also be dipped in chocolate or in melted fondant.

CHAPTER
IV

Fudges

The name fudge is applied to a large group of candies made of sugar boiled with water, milk, or cream, to about 238°F (114.4°C), and stirred or worked with a paddle until candy becomes firm. If stirred while still hot, the resulting candy is coarse and granular. To prevent this, the syrup should be cooled in the saucepan in which it is cooked, or poured out upon a marble slab, platter, or agate tray that has been slightly moistened with a piece of damp cheesecloth. It should not be disturbed until cold. It should then be stirred with a wooden spoon, or worked with a spatula, pushing the spatula forward and lifting up the mass, turning it over and bringing it back, until the whole begins to get stiff. At this stage, turn into a pan, or, better still, leave the candy between bars on the marble slab, regulating the size of the open space according to the amount of candy and the thickness desired.

If the fudge is worked so long that it is too stiff to go smoothly into a pan, return it to a saucepan, and warm slightly over hot water, stirring constantly, until it can be easily poured out. Fudge should be three fourths inch thick, and cut into inch squares. Fudge made with brown sugar is often called penuche. When made with maple sugar or syrup it is called maple fudge or maple cream. Divinity fudge is made by pouring syrup, boiled to 238°F (114.4°C), upon beaten egg whites.

Water, milk, condensed milk diluted with an equal amount of water, thin cream, heavy cream, and sour cream, can all be used for making fudge. With water or skim milk it is desirable to use butter, but this may be omitted when cream is used. With sour cream a few grains of baking soda may be found necessary.

Corn syrup increases the smoothness of the candy. All kinds of nuts, fruits, color pastes, and flavors, as well as the different kinds of sugar, make it possible to produce many varieties of fudge. Opera Fudge is particularly delicious.

Chocolate Fudge I

1 tbsp butter
¾ cup top milk
2 cups sugar
2 squares chocolate
1 tsp vanilla or ¼ tsp cinnamon

Melt butter in saucepan, add sugar, milk, and chocolate, stir gently until chocolate is melted, then bring to boiling point, and boil without stirring to 238°F (114.4°C), or until it will form a soft ball when tried in cold water. Remove candy from fire, and let stand undisturbed until cool, add vanilla or cinnamon, and beat with a wooden spoon; or pour on marble slab and work with a spatula, until candy begins to get sugary. Turn immediately into a buttered pan, and mark in squares with a knife. The pan should be about seven inches square, so that the fudge will be three fourths of an inch thick when cut.

Chocolate Fudge II

2 cups white sugar
1 cup brown sugar
1 cup milk
2 tsp vinegar
2 tbsp butter
2 squares chocolate
1 tsp vanilla

Put sugars and milk in saucepan, stir until sugar is dissolved, and boil without stirring to 238°F (114.4°C), or until candy forms a soft ball when tried in cold water. Add grated chocolate, butter, and vinegar, and pour on marble slab or large platter that has been wiped over with a damp cheesecloth.

When cool add vanilla, and work with a spatula until creamy. Press into a buttered pan, or shape on a marble slab, and when firm cut in squares.

Cocoa Fudge

2 tbsp butter
⅓ cup cocoa
2 cups sugar
½ cup milk
1 tbsp corn syrup
1 tsp vanilla

Put ingredients, except vanilla, into saucepan, bring to boiling point, and boil without stirring to 240°F (115°C), or until candy will form a soft ball when tried in cold water. Remove from fire, leave undisturbed until cool, then beat and stir with a spoon, or work with a spatula, until candy begins to get sugary. Add vanilla, spread in a shallow buttered pan, and mark in squares.

Sour Cream Fudge

2 squares chocolate
⅔ cup sour cream
2 cups sugar
1 tsp vanilla
⅛ tsp salt

Melt the chocolate in saucepan over hot water, add sugar, and when well blended add sour cream slowly. Put on the fire, bring to boiling point, and boil without stirring to 238°F (115.5°C), or until a soft ball is formed when a little candy is tried in cold water. Pour upon a marble slab or platter, slightly moistened by having been wiped over with a piece of damp cheesecloth, and leave undisturbed until cool. Add vanilla and salt, work with spatula or wooden butter paddle until mixture is thick and creamy, then knead with the hands until smooth. Roll out one fourth of an inch thick, and cut out with small fancy cutters.

This fudge may be melted by stirring in a saucepan over hot water. When poured on a loaf of cake it makes a delicious frosting. Satisfactory results may also be obtained by boiling to 230°F (110°C) instead of 238°F (114.4°C).

Chocolate Acorns

White grapes
Chocolate Fudge
Chopped nuts

Remove grapes from bunch, leaving stems as long as possible, and wipe carefully. Melt chocolate fudge over hot water and in it dip grapes, one at a time, holding them by the stem so that about one third is coated. Over this coating sprinkle finely chopped and sifted walnuts. Clip off most of the grape stem. Serve in paper cases.

Chocolate Brazil Nut Fudge

Chocolate Fudge I (p. 47)
1 cup Brazil nuts shelled

Cut one cup of Brazil nut meats in rather large pieces. Make Chocolate Fudge and just before turning it into the pan, stir in the Brazil nuts.

Chocolate Marshmallow Fudge

Chocolate Fudge I (p. 47)
12 marshmallows

Cut marshmallows in pieces. Make Chocolate Fudge, and just before turning it into the pan, fold in the pieces of marshmallow, or place pieces of marshmallow evenly over the surface of the buttered pan, and pour chocolate fudge over them.

Chocolate Walnut Fudge I

Chocolate Fudge I (p. 47)
1 cup walnut meats

Cut one cup of walnut meats in rather large pieces. Make Chocolate Fudge, and just before turning it into the pan, stir in the walnut meats.

Chocolate Walnut Fudge II

2 cups sugar
2 squares chocolate, grated
1 cup rich milk (full fat)
2 tbsp butter
1 cup walnuts

Put sugar and milk in saucepan, stir until sugar is dissolved, and boil without stirring to 238°F (114.4°C), or until candy forms a soft ball when tried in cold water. Add grated chocolate and butter, and pour on marble slab or large platter that has been wiped over with a damp cheesecloth.

When cool, add nut meats, and work with a spatula until creamy. Press into a buttered pan, or shape on a marble slab, and when firm cut in squares.

Condensed Milk Fudge

2 cups sugar
2 squares unsweetened chocolate
¼ cup water
¼ cup condensed milk
2 tbsp butter
1 tsp vanilla

Put sugar, water, milk, and chocolate in saucepan. Heat gradually to the boiling point, and let boil until mixture will form a soft ball when tried in cold water. Remove from range, add butter, pour upon marble slab, and work as other fudges, adding vanilla when mixture is cool.

Cream Nut Ball

2½ squares chocolate
1 tsp vanilla
3 cups sugar
⅛ tsp salt
1 cup sour cream
Chopped nut meats

Put chocolate in saucepan, and melt over hot water. Add sugar and sour cream alternately to chocolate, put directly on range, bring to boiling point, and boil without stirring to 230°F (110°C), or until a very soft ball is formed when candy is tried in cold water.

Pour upon slightly oiled marble slab, large platter, or white agate tray, leave undisturbed until cool, then work with spatula until creamy. Add vanilla and salt, knead with the hands until candy is smooth, shape in small balls or any other desired shape, and roll in chopped nut meats.

Plum Pudding Candy

2 squares chocolate
3 cups sugar
1 cup sour cream
1 tsp vanilla
⅓ cup glacé cherries
⅓ cup Sultana raisins
Few grains cinnamon
1 cup chopped nut meats

Put chocolate in saucepan, and melt over hot water, add sugar and mix well, then add sour cream gradually, stirring it in carefully. Put saucepan on range, bring to boiling point and boil without stirring to 230°F (110°C), or until it forms a very soft ball when tried in cold water. Pour out on slightly dampened marble slab or large platter, and leave undisturbed until cool. Work with a broad spatula until candy gets stiff. Put in a bowl, set bowl over dish of boiling water until candy softens, add cinnamon, vanilla, cherries cut in pieces, raisins, and chopped nut meats; mix well and pour into an oiled brick mold or deep pan. Let stand several days to ripen, remove from mold, and cut in slices.

Sultana Fudge

2 tbsp butter
2 squares chocolate
2 cups sugar
½ cup milk
¼ cup molasses
2 tbsp Sultana raisins
½ cup nut meats
1 tsp vanilla

Melt butter in saucepan, add sugar, molasses, milk, and chocolate, heat gently, and stir until chocolate is melted; then bring to boiling point, and boil without stirring to 238°F (114.4°C), or until candy forms a soft ball when tried in cold water. Remove from fire, leave undisturbed until cool, then beat and stir with a spoon, or work with a spatula, until candy begins to get sugary. Stir in the raisins, nut meats cut in small pieces, and vanilla, pour into a buttered pan, and mark in squares with a knife. English walnuts, hickory or pecan nut meats may be used.

Caramel Fudge

2 cups sugar
⅓ cup boiling water
1 tbsp butter
1 cup milk or cream
1 cup chopped nut meats
Few grains salt

Put one and one third cups sugar in a smooth, hot, iron frying pan and stir with a wooden spoon until sugar melts. Do not allow it to become dark. Add boiling water slowly and simmer until caramelized sugar is entirely melted. Add butter, two thirds cup sugar, and milk; bring to boiling point, and boil to 238°F (114.4°C), or until candy will form a soft ball when tried in cold water. Remove from fire, leave undisturbed until cool, then beat and stir with a spoon, or work with a spatula, until candy begins to get sugary. Stir in the chopped nuts and salt, pour into a buttered pan, and mark in squares. Peanuts, English walnuts, or pecan nuts may be used.

Coconut Fudge

1 tbsp butter
¾ cup milk
2 cups sugar
½ cup shredded coconut
¾ tsp vanilla

Melt butter in saucepan, add sugar and milk, bring to boiling point, and boil without stirring to 238°F (114.4°C), or until candy will form a soft ball when tried in cold water. Remove from fire, leave undisturbed until cool, then beat and stir with a spoon, or work with a spatula, until candy begins to get sugary. Add coconut and vanilla, spread in a shallow buttered pan, and mark in squares.

Coconut Cream Bars

Make Coconut Fudge by preceding recipe, cut in two-inch strips, dip one end in melted coating chocolate, and lay on wax paper or table oil-cloth until chocolate is firm.

Coffee Fudge

3 tbsp butter
1 cup strong coffee
2 cups brown sugar
1 cup nut meats

Melt butter in saucepan, add sugar and coffee, stir until dissolved, bring to boiling point, and boil without stirring to 240°F (115.5°C), or until candy will form a soft ball when a little is tried in cold water. Remove from fire, leave undisturbed until cool, then beat and stir with a spoon, or work with a spatula, until candy begins to get sugary. Add nuts broken in pieces, spread in a shallow buttered pan, and mark in squares.

Coffee Coconut Fudge

4 tbsp dry coffee
½ cup sour cream
⅓ cup water
½ cup shredded coconut
2 cups sugar
½ tsp vanilla
Few grains soda

Put coffee and water in saucepan, bring to the boiling point, then strain through double cheesecloth. To the strained coffee add sugar, cream, and soda, bring to boiling point, and boil without stirring to 238°F (114.4°C), or until candy will form a soft ball when tried in cold water. Remove from fire, leave undisturbed until cool, then beat and stir with a spoon, or work with a spatula, until it begins to get sugary. Stir in shredded coconut and vanilla, spread in a shallow buttered pan, and mark in squares.

Fruit Fudge

3 tbsp butter
1 tbsp corn syrup
1 cup sugar
⅔ cup milk
1 cup brown sugar
1 tsp vanilla
1 cup stoned dates

Melt the butter in saucepan. Add the sugars, corn syrup, and milk, and stir until boiling point is reached. Boil without stirring to 238°F (114.4°C), or until a soft ball is formed when tried in cold water. Pour on a marble slab, large platter, or agate tray, and leave until cool. With a broad spatula scrape and turn the fudge until it begins to get firm. Add the dates and vanilla, mixing them in by kneading mixture with the hands. Shape in smooth, flat cake, half an inch thick, and cut in squares. Raisins, figs, or coconut may be used instead of dates.

Ginger Fudge

½ tbsp butter
2 cups sugar
⅔ cup milk
¼ cup Canton ginger

Melt butter in saucepan, add sugar and milk, bring to boiling point, and boil without stirring to 238°F (114.4°C) or until candy will form a soft ball when tried in cold water. Remove from fire, leave undisturbed until cool, then beat and stir with a spoon, or work with a spatula, until candy begins to get sugary. Add ginger, spread in a shallow buttered pan, and mark in squares.

Marshmallow Fudge I

Use any recipe for fudge, and just before it becomes firm, put half the mixture in a quarter-inch layer in buttered pan or between candy bars. Lay on it a sheet of marshmallow cut the same size, cover with remaining fudge, and leave until firm. Cut in three-quarter-inch squares. If candy becomes too stiff to make smooth layers, put in saucepan, stir over hot water until softened, and use as directed above.

Marshmallow Fudge II

To any recipe for fudge, add three tablespoons marshmallow cream, beat well, and pour into buttered pan or between iron bars. This fudge is always smooth and light in texture.

Maple Marshmallow Fudge

1 tbsp butter
½ cup maple syrup
1 cup sugar
⅓ cup cream
Sheet marshmallow

Melt butter in saucepan, add sugar, syrup, and cream, stir until sugar is dissolved, bring to boiling point, and boil without stirring to 238°F (114.4°C), or until mixture forms a soft ball when tried in cold water. Remove from fire, let stand undisturbed until cool, then beat with a wooden spoon, or pour out on a marble slab or agate tray and work with a spatula, until candy begins to get firm. Return to saucepan, and stir over hot water until melted but not hot. Turn half the mixture in a quarter-inch layer in buttered pan or between candy bars. Lay on it a sheet of marshmallow, cover with remaining fudge, and leave until firm. Cut in three-quarter-inch squares.

Maple Chocolate Fudge

1 tbsp butter
⅓ cup cream
1 cup sugar
2 squares unsweetened chocolate
½ cup maple syrup
½ tsp vanilla

Melt butter in saucepan, add sugar, syrup, cream, and chocolate. Stir gently until chocolate is melted, then bring to boiling point, and boil without stirring to 238°F (114.4°C), or until it will form a soft ball when tried in cold water. Remove candy from fire, and let stand undisturbed until cool. Add vanilla, and beat with a wooden spoon, or pour out on marble slab or agate tray and work with a spatula, until candy begins to get firm. Turn immediately into a buttered pan, or spread between candy bars, and mark in squares with a knife. This may be finished as maple marshmallow fudge, or one cup chopped nuts may be added if desired.

Maple Nut Fudge

1 tbsp butter
⅓ cup cream
1 cup sugar
½ cup maple syrup
1 cup chopped walnuts or pecans
¼ tsp salt

Melt butter in saucepan, add sugar, syrup, and cream, stir until sugar is dissolved, bring to boiling point, and boil without stirring to 238°F (114.4°C), or until mixture forms a soft ball when tried in cold water. Remove candy from fire, and let stand undisturbed until cool. Add nuts and salt, and beat with wooden spoon, or pour out on marble slab and work with spatula, until candy begins to get firm. Turn immediately into a buttered pan, or spread between candy bars and mark in squares.

Pralines

Make recipe for Maple Nut Fudge, omitting nuts. When mixture becomes firm, put in saucepan, stir over hot water until softened, add nuts, preferably pecans, leaving them in large pieces. Drop from spoon on buttered marble slab or tin sheet in rounds three inches in diameter.

Maple Cream

2 cups maple sugar
¾ cup cream or milk

Break sugar in pieces, put in saucepan, add cream or milk, and boil without stirring to 238°F (114.4°C), or until candy will form a soft ball when tried in cold water. Remove from fire, and leave undisturbed until cool. Then stir and beat with a spoon, or work with a spatula, until candy begins to get sugary. Turn into a buttered pan, and mark in squares, or put into very small individual tins. Maple cream may be packed in jelly glasses, covered with paraffin paper and a tin cover, and kept for frosting cake, or used as fondant is used. One cup cream may be used instead of three fourths cup if a richer candy is wanted.

Walnut Maple Cream

To recipe for Maple Cream add three fourths cup walnuts cut in pieces, when candy begins to get sugary.

Pecan Maple Cream

Follow directions for making Maple Cream, adding one cup of pecan nut meats cut in small pieces when candy begins to get sugary.

Hickory nuts or butternuts (white walnut) may be used.

Orange Fudge

2 tbsp butter
Grated rind one orange
2 cups sugar
4 tsp orange juice
¾ cup milk
½ cup candied orange peel

Melt butter in saucepan, add sugar, milk, grated orange rind, and strained orange juice, mix well, bring to boiling point, and boil without stirring to 238°F (114.4°C), or until it will form a soft ball when tried in cold water. Remove from fire, leave undisturbed until cool, then beat and stir with a spoon, or work with a spatula, until candy begins to get sugary. Stir in candied orange peel, cut in small pieces, pour into a buttered pan, and cut in squares.

The recipe for Candied Orange Peel is on page 131. It may be omitted from this recipe if desired.

Peanut Butter Fudge

2 cups sugar
¾ cup milk
4 tbsp peanut butter
1 tsp vanilla
Few grains salt

Put sugar and milk in saucepan, bring to boiling point, and boil without stirring to 238°F (114.4°C), or until candy forms a soft ball when tried in cold water. Remove from fire, let stand undisturbed until cool, add salt, peanut butter, and vanilla; then beat with spoon or work with spatula until creamy; turn into buttered pan and mark in squares.

Raisin Fudge

2 cups light brown sugar
½ cup raisins
⅞ cup thin cream
½ tsp vanilla

Put sugar and cream in saucepan and cook to 238°F (114.4°C), or until a soft ball is formed when tried in cold water. Pour on a marble slab, large platter, or agate tray, and leave until cool. With a broad spatula scrape and turn the fudge until it begins to get firm. When creamy add raisins and vanilla, and spread evenly in a buttered pan, using the hands.

Raspberry Fudge

2 cups sugar
¼ cup raspberry jam
1 cup water
½ tsp raspberry extract
⅛ tsp cream of tartar
Few drops red color paste

Melt butter in saucepan, add sugar and milk, stir until dissolved,
bring to boiling point, and let boil to 238°F (114.4°C), or until a soft
ball is formed when candy is tried in cold water. Remove from fire,
let stand until cool, then add vanilla, and beat until creamy. Turn
into a buttered pan, and cut in squares.

Vanilla Fudge

2⅔ cups confectioners' sugar (icing sugar)
⅔ cup milk
4 tbsp butter
1 tsp vanilla

Melt butter in saucepan, add sugar and milk, stir until dissolved,
bring to boiling point, and let boil to 238°F (114.4°C), or until a soft
ball is formed when candy is tried in cold water. Remove from fire,
let stand until cool, then add vanilla, and beat until creamy. Turn
into a buttered pan, and cut in squares.

Nut Fudge

To Vanilla Fudge add one cup chopped English walnut meats just
before beating the mixture.

Vanilla Opera Fudge

2 cups sugar
1 cup heavy cream (double cream)
⅛ tsp cream of tartar
½ tsp vanilla

Put sugar and cream in saucepan, stir until it boils, add cream of tartar, and boil, stirring carefully to prevent burning, to 238°F (114.4°C), or until candy forms a soft ball when tried in cold water. Move thermometer often, that candy may not burn underneath. Pour on marble slab, agate tray, or large platter which has been slightly moistened with a damp cloth, and leave until cold. With broad spatula or butter paddle work the candy back and forth until it becomes creamy. It may take some time, but it will surely change at last if it was boiled to the right temperature. Cover with a damp cloth for half an hour, then add vanilla, working it in well with the hands. Press into a small shallow box lined with wax paper, let stand to harden, then cut in squares.

Other flavors may be used instead of vanilla, and the candy be tinted with color paste to correspond. Sometimes the fudge is divided into several portions, each flavored and colored differently, and pressed into a box in thin layers, then cut in squares when hard. Or each portion may be packed separately to give more variety when arranged on a bonbon dish.

Assorted Opera Fudges

Variations of Opera Fudge may be secured by omitting vanilla and adding one of the following:

Chopped almonds with almond extract
Chopped candied pineapple with pineapple extract
Candied plums cut in pieces with lemon extract
Chopped candied ginger
Chopped walnuts or pecans with melted chocolate

Rainbow Bar

Prepare recipe for Vanilla Opera Fudge, omitting vanilla, and divide into five portions. Flavor one portion with violet, color with violet color paste, and press into a box lined with wax paper, making a thin layer. On top of the violet, make a thin layer of fudge colored green and flavored with orange flower water. Place on the green a thin layer colored yellow and flavored with lemon; on the yellow a thin layer colored orange and flavored with orange; and on the orange the last portion colored red and flavored with raspberry. When firm, cut in narrow bars.

Maraschino Opera Fudge

2 cups sugar
1 tbsp maraschino cordial
1 cup heavy cream (double cream)
⅛ tsp cream of tartar
⅙ cup candied cherries
⅙ cup citron

Put sugar and cream in saucepan, stir until it boils, add cream of tartar and boil, stirring carefully to prevent burning, to 238°F (114.4°C), or until it forms a soft ball when tried in cold water. Move thermometer often, that candy may not burn underneath.

Pour on a marble slab, agate tray, or large platter which has been slightly moistened with a damp cloth, and leave until cold. With broad spatula or butter paddle work the candy back and forth until it begins to get sugary, add cherries and citron cut in small pieces, and maraschino or other flavor. Continue working until it forms a hard ball, cover with a damp cloth, and leave it for 30 or 40 minutes. Work it with the hands until smooth, and press into a shallow box lined with waxed paper. Let stand to harden, then cut in squares. If the candy is to be sent away, it may be covered with waxed paper and the box cover, without cutting it up.

Orange Flower Opera Fudge

2 cups sugar
4 tsp orange flower water
1 cup heavy cream (double cream)
⅛ tsp cream of tartar
Green color paste
12 marshmallows

Put sugar and cream in saucepan, stir until it boils, add cream of tartar, and boil, stirring carefully to prevent burning, to 238°F (114.4°C), or until it forms a soft ball when tried in cold water. Move thermometer often, that candy may not burn underneath. Pour on a marble slab, agate tray, or large platter which has been slightly moistened with a damp cloth, and leave until cold. With broad spatula or butter paddle work the candy back and forth until it becomes creamy. Cover with a damp cloth for half an hour, then add orange flower water and color paste to make a delicate shade of green. Work with the hands until soft, carefully adding the marshmallows cut in pieces. When evenly mixed, press into a box lined with waxed paper, let stand until firm, and cut in squares.

Pistachio Opera Fudge

2 cups sugar
1 tsp vanilla
1 cup heavy cream (double cream)
⅓ tsp almond extract
⅛ tsp cream of tartar
¼ cup pistachio nuts

Put sugar and cream in saucepan, stir until it boils, add cream of tartar, and boil, stirring carefully to prevent burning, to 238°F (114.4°C), or until it forms a soft ball when tried in cold water. Move thermometer often, that candy may not burn underneath. Pour on a marble slab, agate tray, or large platter which has been slightly moistened with a damp cloth, and leave until cold. With broad spatula or butter paddle work the candy back and forth until it becomes creamy. It may take some time, but it will surely change at last if it was boiled to the right temperature. Cover with a damp cloth for half an hour, add extracts, working them in well with the hands. Put in the pistachio nuts, blanched and cut in pieces, press into a small shallow box lined with waxed paper, let stand to harden, then cut in squares.

Raspberry Opera Fudge

2 cups sugar
1 cup heavy cream (double cream)
⅛ tsp cream of tartar
1 tsp raspberry extract
Scarlet color paste
½ cup blanched almonds

Put sugar and cream in a saucepan, stir until it boils, add cream of tartar, and boil, stirring carefully to prevent burning, to 238°F (114.4°C), or until it forms a soft ball in cold water. Move thermometer often, that candy may not burn underneath. Pour on a marble slab, agate tray, or large platter which has been slightly moistened with a damp cloth, and leave until cold. With broad spatula or butter paddle work the candy back and forth until it becomes firm. Cover with a damp cloth for half an hour, then add extract and color paste to make a delicate shade of pink, working with the hands until creamy. Add almonds cut in pieces, and when well mixed press into a box lined with wax paper. Let stand until firm, and cut in squares. Shredded coconut may be used instead of almonds. Milk or thin cream may be substituted for heavy cream, but candy will not be as soft and rich.

Brown Sugar Fudge or Penuche

2 tbsp butter
¾ cup milk or thin cream
2 cups brown sugar
¾ cup chopped walnuts

Melt butter in saucepan, add sugar and cream, stir until sugar is dissolved, bring to boiling point, and boil without stirring to 238°F (114.4°C), or until candy will form a soft ball when tried in cold water. Remove from fire, leave undisturbed until cool, then beat and stir with a spoon, or work with a spatula, until candy begins to get sugary. Add the walnuts, press into a buttered pan, and mark in squares.

Coconut Penuche

1 tbsp butter
¾ cup cream or milk
2 cups brown sugar
¾ cup shredded coconut
½ tsp vanilla

Melt butter in saucepan, add sugar and cream, stir until dissolved, bring to boiling point, and boil without stirring to 238°F (114.4°C), or until a soft ball is formed when candy is tried in cold water. Remove from fire, leave undisturbed until cool, then beat and stir with a spoon, or work with a spatula, until candy begins to get sugary. Stir in the coconut and vanilla, press into a buttered pan, and mark in squares; or push from tip of spoon upon waxed paper in small round portions.

Fig Penuche

2 tbsp butter
¾ cup milk or thin cream
2 cups brown sugar
¾ cup chopped walnut meats
¾ cup figs cut in pieces

Melt butter in saucepan, add sugar and cream, and stir until dissolved; bring to boiling point, and boil without stirring to 234°F (112.2°C), or until candy will form a very soft ball when tried in cold water. Remove from fire, leave undisturbed until cool, then beat and stir with a spoon or work with a spatula, until candy begins to get sugary. Stir in walnuts and figs, press into a buttered pan, and mark in squares.

Fruit Penuche

2 cups light brown sugar
⅞ cup thin cream
½ cup raisins or dates
½ tsp vanilla

Put sugar and cream in saucepan, bring to boiling point, and boil without stirring to 238°F (114.4°C), or until candy will form a soft ball when tried in cold water. Pour on a marble slab or large platter, and let stand until cool. Work with a spatula until creamy, then add raisins cut in small pieces, and vanilla. Spread evenly in a buttered pan, using the hands, having the mixture three fourths inch deep. When firm, cut in three fourths inch squares.

Marshmallow Penuche

1 tbsp butter
¼ cup milk
2 cups brown sugar
10 marshmallows
Few grains salt
½ cup nut meats

Melt butter in saucepan, add sugar and milk, stir until boiling point is reached, and boil to 230°F (110°C), or until it forms a soft mass that does not dissolve when tried in cold water. Remove from fire, add marshmallows cut in pieces, and pour on marble slab, large platter, or agate tray that has been wiped with a damp cloth.

When cool, add nut meats cut in pieces, and work with a spatula until candy begins to get sugary. Shape in a flat cake on the slab, and when firm, cut in squares.

Pecan Penuche

1 tbsp butter
¾ cup cream or milk
2 cups brown sugar
¾ cup chopped pecan nut meats
⅓ tsp salt

Melt butter in saucepan, add sugar and cream, stir until dissolved, bring to boiling point, and boil without stirring to 238°F (114.4°C), or until a soft ball is formed when candy is tried in cold water.

Remove from fire, leave undisturbed until cool, then beat and stir with a spoon, or work with a spatula, until candy begins to get sugary. Stir in the chopped pecans and salt, press into a buttered pan, and mark in squares; or push from tip of spoon upon waxed paper in small round portions.

Peanut Penuche

Follow directions for Penuche, using three-fourths cup chopped roasted peanuts in place of pecans.

Raisin Penuche

1 cup light brown sugar
¾ cup cream
1 cup confectioners' sugar (icing sugar)
1 tsp vanilla
¼ cup raisins

Put brown sugar, powdered sugar, and cream in saucepan. Stir until mixed, bring to boiling point, and boil without stirring to 238°F (114.4°C), or until candy will form a soft ball when tried in cold water. Remove from fire, leave undisturbed until cool, then beat and stir with a spoon, or work with a spatula until candy begins to get sugary. Stir in the chopped raisins, press into a buttered pan, and mark in squares.

Double Fudge I

Make half the rule of Brown Sugar Fudge (see page 66), and put in buttered pan. Make half the rule of Chocolate Fudge (see page 47), and when it is creamy put in the pan on top of Brown Sugar Fudge. When firm, cut in squares.

Double Fudge II

Make Chocolate Fudge by any of the preceding recipes, and spread half an inch thick in a buttered pan or between bars. Make Pecan Penuche and pour on top. When firm, remove, and cut in squares. Many other combinations may be effectively used.

Divinity Fudge

2 cups sugar
⅓ cup water
⅔ cup corn syrup
2 egg whites
½ cup water
1 tsp vanilla
⅔ cup sugar
⅔ cup chopped nuts

Put two cups sugar, two thirds cup corn syrup, and half a cup of water in saucepan. Put two thirds cup sugar and one third cup water in another saucepan. Cook contents of first saucepan to 240°F (115.5°C), or until mixture forms a soft ball when tried in cold water. 20 minutes after starting this mixture, begin cooking contents of second saucepan, and cook to 255°F (123.9°C), or until mixture forms a hard ball when tried in cold water. Beat whites of eggs until stiff, add contents of first saucepan, and beat constantly until stiff. Then slowly add contents of second saucepan, continuing the beating. Add nut meats and vanilla, turn into a buttered pan, and cut when cold.

Sea Foam Candy

1½ cups light brown sugar
1 tsp vinegar
½ cup cold water
1 egg white
½ cup chopped nuts
½ tsp vanilla

Put sugar, water, and vinegar in saucepan, bring to boiling point, and cook to 240°F (115.5°C), or until candy forms a ball that will just hold its shape when tried in cold water.

Beat white of egg until stiff but not dry, and add the syrup very slowly, while beating constantly. Beat until it begins to get creamy, add nuts and vanilla, and when it will hold its shape, drop in rough lumps on waxed paper, or turn into a buttered pan, and when firm, cut in squares.

If it does not readily become creamy, set dish over hot water, and stir until it begins to get sugary around the edge, then beat until nearly cold, and use as directed above.

Grape-nuts Divinity Fudge

2 cups sugar
1 tsp vanilla
⅓ cup water
1 cup stoned dates
2 egg whites
½ cup grape-nuts

Put sugar and water in saucepan, stir until dissolved, bring to boiling point, and boil without stirring to 238°F(114.4°C), or until syrup will spin a long thread. Beat whites of eggs slightly, then add syrup in a slow, fine stream, beating constantly with a large egg beater, until mixture gets stiff. Add vanilla, dates cut in small pieces, and grape-nuts. Drop from the tip of a teaspoon upon waxed paper, or a buttered platter.

Cherry Puffs

2 cups sugar
⅓ cup water
1 cup corn syrup
Rose color paste
2 egg whites
¼ cup candied cherries
½ tsp vanilla or 1 tsp maraschino

Put sugar, corn syrup, and water in saucepan, stir until dissolved, bring to boiling point, wipe off sugar adhering to sides of saucepan with a butter brush dipped in cold water, and cook syrup to 252°F (122.2°C), or until it forms a hard ball in cold water. With a spoon stir candy slightly until it just begins to look cloudy; slowly, while beating constantly, pour half the syrup on the lightly beaten eggs, then immediately pour the egg mixture into the remaining syrup, and beat.

Add rose color paste to make a delicate pink, then add cherries cut in small pieces, and flavoring. Continue beating until mixture is stiff enough to hold its shape. Push from spoon with a fork on wax paper in little mounds and leave until firm.

Cream Mints

1½ cups sugar
One egg white
¼ cup water
4 drops oil of peppermint or wintergreen
2 tbsp corn syrup (white)
Pink or green color paste

Put sugar, water, and white corn syrup into saucepan. In measuring, use all the syrup that clings to spoon. Stir ingredients until mixed, bring to boiling point and boil without stirring to 238°F (114.4°C), or until syrup will spin a long thread. Have white of egg slightly beaten, and continue beating with egg beater while syrup is being poured in a slow, fine stream upon egg. Continue beating until mixture is stiff enough to keep its shape, using a wooden spoon when mixture becomes too difficult to handle easily with egg beater. Add flavor, color delicately with green or pink color paste, put all the mixture into a pastry bag, and force through a rose tube into separate 'roses' one inch in diameter at the base and one half inch thick in the center. Candy should be soft and creamy, slightly dry, but not coarse or sugary.

FONDANT Candies

Fondant is the foundation of most bonbons and chocolate creams. It is made of sugar cooked with water or other liquid to 238°F (114.4°C). The best results are secured by the use of a thermometer, but if one is not at hand, test the syrup by dipping a spoon into cold water, then into the syrup, and again into the water. Remove candy from spoon with fingers; if it forms a soft ball that will just keep its shape, the syrup is cooked sufficiently. Saucepan should be removed from fire while tests are being made, that candy may not overcook. Another test is to dip spoon into syrup, then lift about twelve inches above saucepan, letting syrup drop from spoon. If it spins a thread at least eight inches long, it has reached the correct stage for fondant, fudge, or ornamental frosting. The addition of an acid to the boiling sugar causes part of the sugar to change to glucose, giving a finer grain to the candy than can be secured without it. Cream of tartar, acetic acid, or vinegar may be used. Corn syrup or glucose takes the place of acid.

When cooked, the syrup is poured on a marble slab, a large platter, or an agate tray which has been moistened by being wiped over with a damp piece of cheesecloth. The candy should stand until it feels cool when tested with the back of the hand. It is then worked with a broad metal spatula, in a sweeping motion forward and backward until candy becomes sugary. The mixture should be continually pushed away and brought back, turning the spatula over with each motion. Candy should be kept all together in a mass while being worked. When it becomes too solid to be moved easily with spatula, it may be kneaded with the hands, as bread is kneaded, until it grows soft and creamy and remains in a compact ball. If it lumps and becomes very hard, it was boiled too long. If it remains too soft to handle, it was not boiled long enough. If too hard, the lumps can sometimes be reduced by persistent kneading, or the mixture can be returned to the saucepan with half a cup of hot water, and reboiled to 238°F (114.4°C). If too soft, confectioners' sugar may be added to make it firm enough to handle, or water can be added, and it can be re-boiled to 238°F (114.4°C). Fondant may be put away in a tightly covered jar, and kept in a cool place for an indefinite time.

White Fondant I

5 cups sugar
1½ cups water
¼ tsp cream of tartar

Put sugar and water in smooth saucepan, place on range, and stir constantly until boiling point is reached. With a damp cloth or a butter brush dipped in cold water, wash down the sides of the saucepan until every grain of sugar is removed. Add cream of tartar, cover saucepan, and allow candy to steam for 3 minutes. Remove cover, put in thermometer, and boil rapidly until candy forms a soft ball when tried in cold water, or until thermometer registers 238°F (114.4°C). While syrup is cooking, wipe marble slab or agate tray with a damp cloth. When syrup is ready, pour gently on the slab. Do not allow the last of it to drip out over what has been poured on the slab, and never scrape out the kettle on the first mixture. Do not disturb the syrup in any way until it is cold. With a spatula or wooden paddle, scrape and turn the syrup toward the center, and continue turning it over and over, working from the edges of the mass. Each time that the syrup is turned over, scrape the slab clean and turn the spatula up and over the mass, occasionally scraping mixture from the spatula with a case knife. It will soon become white and creamy. Knead with the hands until perfectly smooth, cover with a cloth wrung out of cold water, and leave for half an hour. Cut in pieces and put into a stone or glass jar and cover with a wet cloth or glass top. It is better to let it remain two or three days before using, and it may be kept for months in a dry cool place. For making centers and dipping bonbons, see following pages.

White Fondant II

2 cups sugar
½ cup cold water
2 drops acetic acid

Proceed as in White Fondant I, using acetic acid in place of cream of tartar.

White Fondant III

2 cups sugar
½ cup boiling water
⅛ tsp cream of tartar
½ tsp glycerine

Proceed as in White Fondant I, adding glycerine with cream of tartar, when syrup begins to boil.

Butter Fondant

2 cups sugar
1 tsp corn syrup
⅔ cup milk
2 tbsp butter

Put sugar, milk, corn syrup, and butter in saucepan, and proceed as in White Fondant I.

Coffee Fondant

1 cup cold water
2 tbsp ground coffee
2 cups sugar
⅛ tsp cream of tartar

Put water and coffee in saucepan, heat to boiling point, strain through double cheesecloth, add sugar, and proceed as in White Fondant I.

Maple Fondant

1 cup maple sugar
½ cup water
1 cup white sugar
⅛ tsp cream of tartar

Put maple sugar, white sugar, and water in saucepan, and proceed as in White Fondant I.

Opera Fondant

2 cups sugar
1 cup heavy cream
⅛ tsp cream of tartar

Put sugar and cream in saucepan, stir until it boils, add cream of tartar and boil, stirring constantly to prevent burning, but gently so it will not become granular. Cook to 238°F (114.4°C), or until it forms a soft ball when tried in cold water. Pour on marble slab, agate tray, or large platter which has been slightly moistened by wiping it over with a damp cloth, and leave until cold. With a broad metal spatula or a wooden butter paddle bring the edges of the candy into the center, then work candy back and forth with a long sweep of the spatula until it becomes firm. This takes a much longer time than plain fondant to become creamy. Cover with a damp cloth, let stand half an hour, and use as desired. If not wanted at once for fudge, bonbons, or chocolate cream centers, put in glass jar, cover closely, and keep in a cool place.

Assorted Cream Mints

Put plain fondant in upper part of double boiler, and melt over hot water, stirring constantly after fondant begins to soften. Do not allow water to boil or fondant to become hot, as it spoils the gloss. Add flavor and color according to amount of fondant used. Drop from tip of teaspoon on wax paper in rounds one and one quarter inches in diameter, or heat a confectioner's funnel by immersing it in hot water, and push a stick into the small opening. Pour in the melted fondant, and drop on wax paper by raising the stick and lowering it quickly when mint is the right size. In this way a large number of mints may be quickly and evenly molded.

Suggestions for Flavoring and Coloring Cream Mints

Checkermints – color fondant pale pink, and flavor with oil of wintergreen.

Chocolate Mints – add melted chocolate to melted fondant until the right color is obtained, and flavor with vanilla.

Clove Mints – color deep red, and flavor with oil of clove.

Coffee Mints – use coffee fondant.

Lemon Mints – color pale yellow, and flavor with lemon extract.

Lime Mints – color pale green, and flavor with oil of lime.

Maple Mints – use maple fondant. Chocolate, coffee, and maple mints sometimes have a half walnut put in center, held in place with a drop of fondant.

Orange Mints – color orange, and flavor with orange extract.

Peppermints – leave white, and flavor with oil of peppermint.

Raspberry Mints – color deep pink, and flavor with raspberry.

Any of these mints may be dipped in melted fondant of the same color and flavor, or in melted coating chocolate.

Quick Checkermints

2 cups sugar
Pink color paste
¾ cup water
6 drops oil of wintergreen

Put sugar, water, and color paste to make a delicate shade in saucepan, stir until dissolved, and bring to boiling point. Wash down sides of saucepan with a butter brush dipped in cold water, and boil until syrup spins a long thread. Add oil of wintergreen, or half a teaspoon of extract, beat until creamy, and drop from tip of spoon on waxed paper.

When mixture becomes too thick to drop, stir over the fire until it will run again, and drop more mints.

Repeat the warming and dropping until mixture is used.

Quick Peppermints

2 cups sugar
¾ cup boiling water
6 drops oil of peppermint

Put sugar and water in granite saucepan, stir until dissolved, and bring to boiling point. Wash down sides of saucepan with a piece of cheesecloth or a butter brush dipped in cold water, and boil until syrup spins a long thread. Add peppermint, beat until creamy, and drop from tip of spoon on waxed paper. When mixture becomes too thick to drop, stir over the fire until it will run. Continue dropping and reheating until mixture is used.

Center Cream I

2 cups sugar
⅓ cup corn syrup
½ cup cold water

Put sugar, corn syrup, and cold water in saucepan, and proceed as in White Fondant I (page 75). The fondant may be worked before it becomes perfectly cold, and should be put in a jar before it becomes firm, as it is very sticky if left under a wet cloth and kneaded. This makes a soft smooth cream, and is best used by being molded in cornstarch, and coated with chocolate. Be very careful not to get it hot when melting it, or the centers will be hard, instead of creamy.

Center Cream II

2 cups sugar
¼ tsp cream of tartar
½ cup hot water
1 egg white
½ tsp vanilla

Put sugar, water, and cream of tartar in saucepan, stir until mixed, and bring quickly to boiling point. Wash down sides of saucepan with a piece of cheesecloth or a butter brush dipped in cold water, removing every crystal, and rinsing brush in water as needed. If crystals remain, they are likely to make the fondant grainy. Cover until it has boiled 2 minutes, remove cover, put in candy thermometer, and cook to 236°F (113.3°C), or until it forms a soft ball when tried in cold water. Pour on a marble slab, large platter, or white agate tray that has been slightly moistened by being wiped with a damp cloth, and let stand undisturbed until candy is nearly cool. Beat egg until stiff, pour on top of candy, add vanilla, and work with broad spatula until very white and creamy. Just before it begins to set, turn it over and over very slowly, working from the edge. When firm, shape at once into small balls, working chopped nuts into it if desired. Drop into confectioners' sugar, rolling around until ball is thoroughly covered, lay on waxed paper, and dip at once in melted chocolate. This center cream may be melted over hot water and molded in starch as on page 81 if desired, but centers will not be quite as soft and creamy.

Maple Center Cream

1½ cups maple sugar
¾ cup white sugar
¼ tsp glycerine
3 drops acetic acid
1 cup water
1 egg white

Put both kinds of sugar and the water in saucepan, stir until dissolved, add glycerine, and stir again. Wash down sides of saucepan with a piece of cheesecloth or a butter brush dipped in cold water, removing every crystal. Add acetic acid, cover, and boil 2 minutes. Remove cover, and boil to 238°F (114.4°C), or until it forms a soft ball when tried in cold water. Finish like Center Cream II.

BONBONS

The name bonbon is given commercially to a candy that is from one to one and one half inches in diameter, and has an outside coating of fondant, and a center of fondant or other candy, with or without nuts and fruit.

Fondant centers are most commonly used, and their preparation is not difficult. Many other kinds of centers may also be coated with fondant, and with different kinds of fondant coating and a few decorations, a large variety of bonbons may be readily secured. The following pages contain many suggestions for making bonbons.

Centers for Bonbons

Bonbon centers may be made from any of the fondants or creams given in this chapter or the chapter on Uncooked Candies. Remove the desired amount of fondant from the jar in which it was put to ripen, and color and flavor as suggested below. If firm enough, shape in small balls with a piece of nut, cherry, or other fruit in the center. Leave on a board covered with wax paper until firm enough to dip. It is sometimes wise to let them remain overnight. If too soft to shape, as Center Cream I and II may be, put in a double boiler over hot water, and stir constantly until thin enough to pour. It should be warm but not hot. Prepare starch molds as explained below. A small piece of nut, cherry, or other fruit may be put in each mold. Put the melted fondant into the impressions in the starch, and leave until firm. Remove from starch, and centers are ready to dip.

To Mold in Cornstarch

Sift cornstarch lightly into a shallow cake pan placed in a large pan or tray. Very gently level off the top with a long stick, knife, or ruler. Make impressions in the starch with small plaster molds bought for the purpose from a confectioners' supply house, and fastened to a strip of wood; or with the handle of a knife, a thimble, or other object of the desired size. In making impressions, the molds each time must be slightly pushed away from the preceding impressions, that they may not be disturbed. Pour the liquid candy into the impressions with a teaspoon, or pour candy into a warmed confectioner's funnel, and let it run out into the impressions, checking it by lowering into the opening the stick that comes with the funnel. Leave until firm, remove candies from cornstarch into a large sifter, shake well, and remove remaining starch with a clean brush.

A cheap grade of cornstarch may be provided, and if kept in a closed jar or tin, it may be used over and over again. Flour may be used instead of cornstarch if more convenient, but it is not so satisfactory.

Dipping Bonbons

Put the desired amount of fondant in small saucepan or double boiler, set in a larger saucepan of hot water, and stir constantly until melted. Flavor and color as suggested below. Add a few drops of cold water if necessary, to make it thin enough for dipping. The fondant should not be allowed to become hot. Have tray of centers on table at the left, piece of waxed paper on board or tray at right, and the fondant, over hot water, between. With the left hand drop one center at a time into the melted fondant. With a candy dipper, in the right hand, stir until center is entirely covered, then lift up, and put on paper, making a coil on top of each bonbon with the dipper. The whole process of dipping must be done as quickly as possible, and the fondant must be stirred frequently. When the fondant becomes too thick, add a few drops of cold water, and stir well. Occasionally put back on the fire until the water boils underneath. Chopped nuts, a bit of cherry, ginger, or other decoration may be put on top of each bonbon before the fondant hardens. Many suggestions for centers and decorations are given on the following pages.

More fondant should be melted than is required for dipping, that the center may be rolled about and completely covered. The remainder, after all the centers are coated, may be remelted and dropped from a spoon on waxed paper in rounds the size of a half dollar, or be poured into a small buttered pan, and when firm, cut in squares; or shredded coconut may be mixed with it, and it can be dropped in rough heaps on wax paper.

Coloring Fondant

When coloring is to be added to plain fondant, take a small portion of color paste on the end of a toothpick, and mix with a small portion of fondant, then mix, a little at a time, with the remaining fondant, using a spatula, until the desired shade is secured. Care should be taken that color is not too deep, as light shades only are desirable for candies.

Suggestions for Color and Flavor for Fondant Centers, or Fondant Coating

Put the desired amount of fondant in small saucepan or double boiler

Chocolate
>Vanilla flavor

Green
>Oil of lime
>Orange flower water
>Vanilla three parts, almond one part

Lavender
>Violet flavour

Light brown
>Brown sugar and vanilla
>Coffee flavour
>Maple flavor

Orange
>Grated orange rind
>Orange extract

Pink
>Raspberry flavor
>Rose flavor
>Strawberry flavor
>Wintergreen

White
>Almond flavor
>Candied fruits
>Maraschino flavor
>Peppermint flavor
>Vanilla flavor

Yellow
>Lemon flavor

Suggestions for Centers for Bonbons, to be Used Alone or Mixed with Fondant Flavored and Colored Appropriately

Apricot paste
Candied fruit
>Cherries
>Citron, small pieces
>Ginger, small pieces
>Limes, small pieces
>Pears, small pieces
>Pineapple, small pieces
>Plums, small pieces

Candied mixed fruit, chopped
Canned pineapple, well dried and served at once in paper cases
Caramels, half size, any kind
Dried fruits
>Dates, small pieces
>Dates, stuffed and cut in pieces
>Figs, chopped
>Figs, small pieces
>Prunes, two tablespoons mixed with one fourth cup each cherries and nuts, all finely chopped
>Raisins
>Raisins, stuffed with chopped nuts

Fresh fruits, served at once in paper cases
>Grapes, white, Malaga, or Tokay
>Oranges, small sections
>Strawberries, hulls on

Fudge, small pieces, any kind
Greengage paste
Guava jelly
Marshmallows
Mint jelly
Nuts
>Almond paste
>Almonds, plain
>Almonds, salted
>Almond paste, mixed with twice the amount of fondant

      Brazil nuts, in pieces
      Brazil nuts, whole
      Coconut, mixed with fondant
      Peanuts
      Peanut brittle, chopped
      Peanut butter
      Pecans
      Walnuts, halved, plain
      Walnuts, halved, salted
Penuche, small pieces, any kind
Two parts cherries and one part citron, chopped and mixed

Suggestions for Decorations on Top of Bonbons

Almonds, blanched and halved
Candied
      Angelica
      Cherry, small piece
      Ginger, small piece
      Mint leaves
      Pineapple, small piece
      Rose leaves
      Violet
Coconut
      Plain
      Colored
Pecans
Pistachio nuts
      Chopped
      Whole
Silver dragées
Tiny candies
Walnuts
      Chopped
      Whole

Opera Bonbons

Color and flavor as desired small portions of Opera Fondant. With the hands shape in small balls, putting a piece of nut, cherry, or marshmallow in the center of each ball.

Melt another portion of Opera Fondant in a double boiler over hot water, stirring constantly. Add half a teaspoon of vanilla, and drop centers one at a time in the fondant. Remove with candy dipper or two-tined fork to waxed paper. When enough white bonbons have been made, add a little pink or green color paste and raspberry or almond extract to taste to the melted fondant. Dip more of the centers, stirring the fondant, and reheating it if it becomes too stiff. Then add to remaining fondant one square melted chocolate, and dip remaining balls. In this way a great variety of attractive bonbons may be produced. Other flavors and colors may be used for greater variety, and tops may be decorated with small pieces of nuts or cherries if desired. The centers may also be dipped in melted coating chocolate. White Fondants I, II, or III (page 75–6) may be used instead of Opera Fondant.

Coconut Centers

4½ tbsp sugar
3 tbsp corn syrup
1½ cups shredded coconut
1 tsp butter
¼ cup water
1 tsp vanilla

Put sugar, corn syrup, and water in saucepan, and stir until mixture boils. Wash down sides of saucepan with a butter brush dipped in cold water, and cook to 238°F (114.4°C), or until mixture forms a soft ball when tried in cold water. Remove from fire, add coconut, butter, and vanilla, and stir just enough to mix the ingredients but not enough to cause it to become sugary. When well mixed spread on marble slab or platter, and when cold mold into small balls and lay on wax paper. Dip in melted fondant or melted coating chocolate.

Coconut Bonbons

Dip Coconut Centers in melted colored fondant, then roll in coconut colored the same as the fondant.

To Color Coconut

Sprinkle shredded coconut on a sheet of white paper. Add a little color paste diluted with a few drops of water, and rub evenly through the coconut. Dry slowly, and store in covered glass jars. Colored coconut may be used on the outside of bonbons, creams, stuffed dates, and frosted cakes.

Marshmallow Mint Bonbons

Marshmallows Fondant
Oil of peppermint
Ornamental frosting

Cut marshmallows in two crosswise, and flavor each piece by touching the cut surface with a small wooden skewer which has been dipped into a bottle of oil of peppermint. Arrange marshmallows in layers in a box, cover, and let stand overnight. Melt fondant by stirring in a saucepan over hot water, dip each piece separately, lay on waxed paper, and when all are dipped decorate if desired with tiny flowers made by forcing ornamental frosting through paper tubes. (See Chapter XVI.)

Violet Marshmallow Bonbons

Cut marshmallows in halves, dip in fondant flavored with violet extract and colored delicately with violet color paste. Put on wax paper, and decorate tops with a piece each of candied violet and angelica before fondant becomes firm.

Philadelphia Bonbons

Dip bonbon centers made of Center Cream I or II (page 80) in melted fondant to which has been added chopped candied cherries, candied pineapple, nuts, dates, or figs, and drop on wax paper.

Fondant Acorns

Maple fondant
Blanched almonds

Make centers of maple fondant the size and shape of small acorns. When dry dip in maple fondant, melted by stirring it in a saucepan over hot water. When all are dipped, beginning with the first one, dip the base again in melted fondant and then in finely chopped almonds.

Plain fondant, tinted green and flavored with almond, may be used instead of maple fondant, and the base dipped in chopped pistachio nuts.

Creamed Fruits

Candied fruits
Fondant

Put fondant in saucepan, add a few drops vanilla, and set over another saucepan of boiling water. Stir until melted, but not hot. Dip candied cherries, or pieces of candied pineapple, pears, or plums in the melted fondant, decorate top with a small piece of fruit, dry on waxed paper, and serve in paper cases.

Creamed Grapes

Malaga or Tokay grapes
Fondant

Remove grapes from bunch, leaving stems as long as possible. Wipe carefully, dip one at a time in fondant that has been melted by stirring it in a saucepan over hot water, and place grapes on waxed paper to dry. Serve in paper cases.

Creamed Strawberries

Fresh strawberries
Fondant

Wipe selected strawberries, dip one at a time in fondant that has been melted by stirring it in a saucepan over hot water, and place strawberries on waxed paper to dry. Serve in paper cases.

Creamed Marzipan

Almond paste
Walnuts
Egg white
Fondant

To almond paste add egg white, a very little at a time, and work with a spatula until it is of the right consistency to shape. Form into small balls, press half a nut meat on each side of each ball, and dip in melted fondant colored and flavored as desired.

Creamed Marzipan Blocks

Almond paste
Grated orange rind
Egg white
Rose color paste
Orange color paste
Raspberry extract
½ cup sugar
¼ cup water
Melted fondant
Paper cases

To almond paste add white of egg, a very little at a time, and work with a spatula until it is of right consistency to shape. Divide in three portions; to one add rose color paste to make a deep pink, and a few drops of raspberry extract. To another portion add grated orange rind and orange color paste to make a good color. Roll pieces on slab, with rolling pin, one fourth inch thick and the same shape.

Boil sugar and water until syrup spins a thread. Brush pink layer of paste with syrup, cover with plain layer of paste, brush with syrup, and cover with orange layer. Press under a light weight, cut in cubes, dip in melted fondant, and serve in paper cases.

Glacé Nut Creams

Glacé nuts
Vanilla
Fondant
Almond extract
Green color paste

Prepare glacé pecans or walnuts (see page 122). Flavor a small portion of fondant with one quarter teaspoon vanilla and a few drops almond extract, and color green. Make into small balls, and press between two glacéd nuts. Keep in a cold place, and use if possible the day they are made.

Nut Caramel Rolls

Cut a sheet of Vanilla Caramel that is three eighths of an inch thick into strips three eighths of an inch wide and one inch long. Dip in melted fondant, and roll at once in finely chopped walnut meats. Candy, when covered with fondant, should be one and one half inches long.

Plum Creams

4 canned plums
Confectioners' sugar (icing sugar)
Fondant
Maraschino cordial

Force plums through a sieve, and add confectioners' sugar to make a stiff paste. Shape in small balls, dry on waxed paper, and dip in melted fondant flavored with maraschino cordial.

CARAMELS and Nougatines

When sugar mixtures are boiled to 242°F (116.7°C) and up to 250°F (121.1°C), and are not beaten after cooking, they are soft and waxy. When removed from the fire, they should be of the consistency desired in the finished candy. Longer boiling makes the candies too hard. Cream and corn syrup are used in the best caramels, and with different flavors, nuts, fruits, or marshmallow, the various varieties found in the shops may be easily duplicated.

Nougatines are similar to caramels with beaten whites of eggs added to give a porous consistency, and usually nuts or combinations of nuts and fruits are used. Rice paper is put on the top and bottom of nougatines, and may be eaten with the candy without harm.

Except in very cold weather, caramels and nougatines should be wrapped in wax paper as soon as cut, or dipped in melted coating chocolate or fondant.

Vanilla Caramels

1 cup sugar
½ cup corn syrup
1½ cups cream
1 tsp vanilla

Put sugar, corn syrup, and half a cup of cream in saucepan, stir until sugar is dissolved, bring to boiling point, and boil until mixture will form a soft ball when tried in cold water. Stir gently and constantly to prevent burning, making the spoon reach all parts of the bottom of the saucepan. Do not beat, as beating may cause the candy to become granular. As soon as candy forms a soft ball add another half cup of cream. Boil until it again forms a soft ball in cold water, add remaining cream, and boil until candy will form a decidedly firm ball when tried in cold water. The caramels when cold will be of the same consistency as this firm ball. Pour caramel into a buttered pan seven inches square. When cool cut in squares, and wrap in wax paper. If caramel should get sugary, return it to kettle, add more cream, and boil again. If all the cream is added at once, caramels may be made in a shorter time, but they will not be as rich and creamy.

Coconut Caramels

To Vanilla Caramel mixture add one cup coconut just before pouring
it into the buttered pan.

Nut Caramels

To Vanilla Caramel mixture add one cup nut meats just before pouring it into the buttered pan.

Raspberry Caramels

To Vanilla Caramel mixture add four teaspoons raspberry extract
and rose color paste to make the right tint, before pouring it into the
buttered pan.

Fruit Caramels

To Vanilla Caramel mixture add eight figs or three fourths cup raisins cut
in pieces, just before pouring it into the buttered pan.

Marshmallow Caramels

To Vanilla Caramel mixture add sixteen marshmallows cut in pieces,
before pouring into buttered pan.

Marshmallow Layer Caramels

Prepare any recipe for caramels and pour half the mixture one fourth
inch deep in a buttered pan or between candy bars. Cover with a piece
of sheet marshmallow cut the same size, and pour remaining caramel
mixture over the marshmallow one fourth inch deep. When firm, cut in
three quarter inch cubes and wrap in wax paper.

Chocolate Caramels I

Make Vanilla Caramels, and with the last half cup of cream add three squares grated chocolate. Finish as Vanilla Caramels.

Chocolate Almond Caramels

To Chocolate Caramels add one cup blanched almonds before pouring into buttered pan.

Pine Nut Caramels

Follow directions for Chocolate Caramels, adding one cup salted pine nuts before pouring into buttered pan.

Chocolate Caramels II

½ cup white sugar
½ cup brown sugar
½ cup molasses
3 squares chocolate, grated
1 cup cream or milk
1 tsp vanilla
1 tsp soda
½ tsp salt
2 tbsp butter
1 cup whole nut meats

In a saucepan put white sugar, brown sugar, and molasses, bring to the boiling point, add grated chocolate and one third of the milk. Stir gently to mix the ingredients. Let boil until it begins to thicken, and add one third cup milk, stir again, allow mixture to boil until it thickens, and add remaining milk. Stir gently and constantly, that candy may not burn (do not beat, as beating may cause candy to become granular), and boil until candy forms a firm ball when tried in cold water. This will be about 242°F (116.7°C). Add vanilla, soda, salt, butter, and nut meats. Turn into buttered pan, and when cold cut in three fourths inch squares. Caramel should be three fourths inch deep in pan.

This caramel requires a long time in cooking, and when taken from the fire should be as firm (when tried in cold water) as it is wanted when ready to eat.This caramel requires a long time in cooking, and when taken from the fire should be as firm (when tried in cold water) as it is wanted when ready to eat.

Brown Sugar Caramels

2½ tbsp butter
½ cup milk
2 cups brown sugar
2 tbsp molasses
4 squares unsweetened chocolate
1 tsp vanilla

Put butter in saucepan, and when melted add sugar, molasses, and milk. Bring to the boiling point, add chocolate, and stir constantly until chocolate is melted. Let boil until mixture forms a firm ball when tried in cold water. Add vanilla, turn into a buttered tin, cool slightly, and cut in squares.

Molasses Chocolate Caramels

3 tbsp butter
1 cup molasses
¾ cup cream
1 cup sugar
4 squares unsweetened chocolate
½ tsp vanilla

Melt butter in a Scotch kettle, and add cream, sugar, and molasses. Bring to the boiling point, and add chocolate, balancing it on a large wooden spoon that it may melt gradually with no danger of burning on the kettle. Continue the boiling, stirring occasionally, until a firm ball may be formed when mixture is tried in cold water. Add vanilla, and turn into a buttered pan, having the mixture three fourths inch in depth. When nearly cold, cut in cubes, using scissors or a sharp knife. Wrap in squares of wax paper, and let stand in a cold place to harden.

Nut Chocolate Caramels

To Molasses Chocolate Caramels add one cup blanched and chopped almonds or chopped English walnut meats, just before taking from fire.

Stretched Chocolate Caramels

2 cups sugar
2 tsp glycerine
2 cup boiling water
1½ squares unsweetened chocolate
⅓ tsp cream of tartar
2 tbsp heavy cream (double cream)

Put first four ingredients in saucepan, bring to the boiling point and let boil, without stirring, until mixture will become brittle when tried in cold water. When nearly cooked, add cream and chocolate. Turn on a buttered platter, and as edges cool, fold towards center. As soon as cool enough to handle, pull until glossy, and cut into small pieces, using knife or scissors. Put on wax paper or on slightly buttered plate.

Caramels with Evaporated Milk

1½ cups sugar
1½ cups corn syrup
1½ cups rich milk (full fat)
1½ cups evaporated milk
1 cup nuts

Mix the evaporated milk with the plain milk, and put one and a half cups of the mixture with sugar and corn syrup in a saucepan, and stir and cook until it will form a soft ball when tried in cold water. Continue stirring, and add slowly three fourths cup of the milk, cook again until it forms a soft ball, then slowly add remaining milk, stirring constantly all over the bottom of the saucepan so that candy will not stick. The fire should not be too hot, as the mixture burns easily. When it forms a firm ball of the consistency you wish for your caramels, remove from fire, add vanilla, and any kind of nuts you prefer. Scrape out into buttered pan, and cut when cold. Wrap in wax paper if desired.

Maple Caramels

⅔ cup maple sugar
⅔ cup white sugar
½ cup corn syrup
2 cups cream

Put sugar, corn syrup, and half a cup cream in saucepan, stir until sugar is dissolved, bring to boiling point, and boil until mixture will form a soft ball when tried in cold water. Stir gently and constantly to prevent burning, making the spoon reach all parts of the bottom of the saucepan. Do not beat, as beating may cause the candy to become granular. As soon as candy forms a soft ball, add another half cup of cream. Boil until it again forms a soft ball in cold water, add remaining cream, and boil until candy will form a decidedly firm ball when tried in cold water. The caramels when cold will be of the same consistency as this firm ball. Pour caramel into a buttered pan seven inches square. When cool, cut in squares, and wrap in wax paper. If caramel should get sugary, return it to kettle, add more cream and boil again. If all the cream is added at once, caramels may be made in a shorter time, but they will not be as rich and creamy as when cream is added at three different times.

Nougatines I

½ cup corn syrup
½ cup hot water
2 cups sugar
2 egg whites
½ cup nut meats
1 tsp vanilla

Put corn syrup, hot water, and sugar in saucepan, stir until sugar is dissolved, and boil without stirring to 270°F (132.2°C), or until candy is brittle when tried in cold water. Beat the egg whites stiff, and add the syrup gradually, beating mixture until creamy. Add vanilla, and when almost firm, add chopped nut meats.

Pour into pan lined with rice paper, cover with a sheet of rice paper, and leave until firm. Cut in pieces one and one half inches long and five eighths of an inch wide and thick. Wrap in wax paper, or dip in melted coating chocolate.

Nougatines II

1 cup granulated sugar
⅓ cup corn syrup
⅓ cup honey (strained)
¼ tsp paraffin (melted)
2 egg white
¼ tsp salt
¼ cup water
½ cup blanched almonds
¼ cup cherries
¼ cup blanched pistachio nuts
1 tsp vanilla

Put the sugar, corn syrup, honey, paraffin, and water in saucepan, stir occasionally, and let boil to the hard ball degree, about 248°F (120°C). Add the salt to the eggs, beat until dry, and gradually pour on part of the syrup, beating constantly meanwhile with the egg beater; return the rest of the syrup to the fire, and let boil until it is brittle when tested in cold water, or to 290°F (143.3°C). Then turn this gradually on the eggs, beating constantly.

Return the whole to the saucepan, set over the fire on a very heat-proof mat, and beat until it becomes crisp when tested in cold water. Add nuts and cherries, cut in pieces, and vanilla. Pour into a buttered pan a little larger than an ordinary bread pan, lined with rice paper. Set aside to become cold, and cut into pieces about an inch and a quarter long and three eighths of an inch wide and thick. Wrap in wax paper, or dip in melted coating chocolate.

Quick Nougatines

1 cup marshmallows
½ cup almond paste
¼ cup pistachio nuts
¼ cup candied cherries

Put marshmallows and almond paste in double boiler, and stir and
heat until melted and well blended. Add nuts and cherries cut in
small pieces, and spread half an inch thick on a pan or slab sprinkled
with confectioners' sugar. When firm, cut in bars one and one half
inches long and half an inch wide. Dip if desired in melted fondant
or coating chocolate.

Esmeralda Cream

2 cups sugar
⅔ cup white corn syrup
3 tbsp cold water
2 egg whites
1½ cups nut meats
¾ tsp vanilla
Few drops almond extract

Put sugar, corn syrup, and water in saucepan, stir until well mixed,
heat gradually to boiling point, and boil without stirring to 260°F
(126.7°C), or until it begins to crack in cold water. Beat egg whites
until they are light and frothy, but not stiff and dry; continue beating
with an egg beater while the syrup is being poured in a fine steady
stream on the egg. Beat until mixture is stiff enough to hold its shape.
A wooden spoon may be used when mixture begins to stiffen. Add
nut meats, cut in large pieces, and flavoring, turn into a deep pan
lined with wafer paper, cover top with wafer paper, and when nearly
cold turn from pan, and cut into oblong pieces. Wrap each piece
in wax paper. For nuts a mixture of English walnuts, almonds, and
pistachio nuts may be used. A few candied cherries cut in quarters
may be added if desired.

CHAPTER VII

PULLED Candies

Candies that are to be pulled need to be boiled to 254°F (123.3°C) or up to 260°F (124.4°C). When removed from the fire they should be of the consistency required for the finished candy. A bit of paraffin keeps the candy from sticking to the teeth when being chewed, but it is not digestible, and its use in manufactured candies is forbidden in several States.

Molasses candies need to be stirred during the last part of the cooking to prevent burning.

A candy hook attached to the wall is convenient when much candy is to be pulled.

If, while being pulled, candy sticks to the hands, they may be rubbed with flour.

Molasses Candy

3 tbsp butter
⅔ cup sugar
2 cups Porto Rico molasses
1 tbsp vinegar

Melt butter in saucepan or iron kettle, add molasses and sugar, and stir until sugar is dissolved. Boil until mixture becomes brittle when tried in cold water, or to 256°F (124.4°C). During the last part of the cooking candy should be stirred constantly. Add vinegar just before taking from fire. Pour on buttered marble slab or agate tray, and when cool enough to handle, pull until porous and light colored, using tips of fingers and thumbs, not squeezing it in the hand. Cut in small pieces, using large scissors or a sharp knife. Wrap in wax paper.

Daddy's Molasses Candy

1 cup molasses
½ cup sugar
1 tsp soda

Put molasses and sugar in saucepan or iron kettle. Stir until dissolved, and boil without stirring over a moderate fire, brushing inside edge of saucepan with butter to prevent boiling over. Cook to 256°F (124.4°C), or until mixture spins fine threads when dripped slowly from tip of spoon.

Put three tablespoons of candy into a buttered dish, and keep in a warm place for coloring. Add soda to remaining candy, stir, and turn into buttered pan or on to buttered slab. When cool enough to handle, pull as quickly and as long as possible. When very light, lay upon it the unpulled candy, and pull out together in one long strip. Cut in small pieces, and roll in confectioners' sugar. If candy is not to be eaten at once, wrap each piece in waxed paper.

Stretched Molasses Candy

3 tbsp butter
⅓ cup butter
1⅓ cups sugar
⅔ cup molasses
1 cup water

Put butter in saucepan or iron kettle, and when melted add sugar, molasses, and water. Stir until sugar is dissolved, and let boil without stirring until mixture will form a very soft ball that will just keep in shape when tried in cold water. Turn on a buttered marble slab or agate tray, and as mixture cools around sides fold toward center. When cool enough to handle, pull until porous and light colored with tips of fingers and thumbs, not squeezing it in the hand. Cut in small pieces with large scissors or a sharp knife, and arrange on slightly buttered plates, or wrap in wax paper. A few drops oil of peppermint, clove, or cinnamon may be added during the stretching.

Molasses Kisses

2 tbsp butter
3 tbsp honey
¼ cup water
1 tbsp corn syrup
1 cup molasses
3 tbsp sugar

Put ingredients in saucepan or iron kettle, stir until butter melts and sugar dissolves, and boil until it forms a hard ball in cold water, or to 254°F (123.3°C) or 256°F (124.4°C). Pour gently on buttered marble slab or large tray. When cool enough to handle, pull until light colored. If using the hook, twist each time as it falls from the hook. Use flour on the hands if candy sticks. Roll, cut in pieces, and wrap in wax paper.

Molasses Candy Bars

Follow directions for Molasses Kisses, cooking to 256°F (124.4°C). Pull as long a time as possible, then cut in bars, and wrap in wax paper.

Velvet Molasses Kisses

½ cup molasses
1½ tbsp vinegar
1½ cups sugar
½ cup water
¼ tsp cream of tartar
4 tbsp butter
⅛ tsp soda

Put molasses, sugar, water, and vinegar in saucepan or iron kettle, stir until it boils, and add cream of tartar. Boil until mixture becomes brittle when tried in cold water, or to 256°F (124.4°C).

Stir constantly during last part of cooking. When nearly done, add butter and soda. Pour on buttered marble slab or agate tray, and when cool pull until light colored. While pulling, flavor with one teaspoon vanilla, or half a teaspoon of lemon extract, or a few drops oil of peppermint or wintergreen. Cut in pieces with scissors, and wrap in wax paper.

Taffy

1½ tbsp butter
1 cup sugar
⅔ cup corn syrup
⅓ cup water

Melt the butter in saucepan, add sugar, corn syrup, and water, and stir until sugar is dissolved, bring to boiling point, and boil without stirring to 260°F (126.6°C), or until it forms a hard ball when tried in cold water. Pour on a marble slab or white agate tray which has been slightly moistened by being wiped over with a piece of damp cheesecloth. Fold edges over into the center before they have time to get hard; by doing this the candy will be kept soft, but in doing it the candy must be disturbed as little as possible, as any tendency toward stirring it may cause it to sugar, and then it cannot be pulled. As soon as candy is cool enough to handle, knead it until firm, add flavor, then pull it over a hook until it is white. Cut with scissors into bars, and wrap in waxed paper.

Salt Water Taffy

1½ cups brown sugar
½ cup water
½ cup corn syrup
3 tbsp butter
1½ tsp salt
½ tbsp glycerine
1½ tsp vanilla

Put brown sugar, corn syrup, butter, and water in saucepan or iron kettle, and boil, stirring occasionally, to 256°F (124.4°C), or until it forms a hard ball when tried in cold water. Add salt and glycerine, pour on greased marble slab or agate tray, and when cool enough to handle, pull until light colored. Add vanilla while pulling. Pull out in round sticks the size of kisses, cut in small pieces with scissors, and wrap in waxed paper.

Atlantic City Salt Water Taffy

1 cup sugar
½ tbsp cornstarch
1 tbsp butter
½ cup water
⅔ cup corn syrup
½ tsp salt
Flavoring

Mix sugar and cornstarch, put in saucepan, add corn syrup, butter, and water. Stir until boiling point is reached, and boil to 256°F (124.4°C), or until it forms a firm ball when tried in cold water. Add salt, pour on greased slab or agate tray, and when cool enough to handle, pull until light colored. Divide in separate portions, and color and flavor each portion as desired, while it is being pulled. Lemon, orange, peppermint, lime, strawberry, or pineapple flavors may be used, and pink, green, yellow, or orange color paste.

To make red striped kisses have one portion of candy colored bright red and kept warm near the oven. Lay the large piece of pulled taffy on the slab; on the upper side lay two or three parallel strips of red taffy; turn the piece over and lay two or three red strips on that side. Pull out until one and one half inches wide and three fourths inch thick. Cut in pieces with scissors, and wrap in wax paper.

After Dinner Mints

2 cups sugar
¼ tsp cream of tartar
⅔ cup boiling water
1 tsp vinegar
Few drops oil of peppermint

Put sugar, water, cream of tartar, and vinegar in a saucepan, and mix ingredients thoroughly.

Bring to the boiling point, and boil without stirring to 265°F (124.4°C), or until mixture will become brittle when tried in cold water. Pour on an oiled marble slab, or large white agate tray, and leave undisturbed until cool enough to handle easily. Lift candy, avoiding any movement that is like a stirring motion, as stirring may cause candy to sugar, and pull, doubling candy over evenly and pulling out as long as possible, keeping the grain all one way. Add flavoring during the pulling. When candy is too stiff to pull longer, stretch out into a long rope, half an inch in diameter, and cut with scissors into small pieces. Put immediately into a bowl of confectioners' sugar (icing sugar), stir until well coated, and when dry put into a glass jar, cover, and let stand several days in a warm place, when candies should become tender and sugary.

Candy may be divided into several portions, and one portion colored pink and flavored with wintergreen; another portion may be colored green and flavored with almond and vanilla; another portion may be colored yellow and flavored with lemon or orange.

Peppermint Stick Candy

2 cups sugar
¼ cup corn syrup
½ cup water

Put sugar, corn syrup, and water in saucepan, stir until sugar is dissolved, bring to boiling point, and boil without stirring to 310°F (154.4°C), or until it begins to discolor on edge of saucepan.

Pour out on oiled marble slab or platter, cut off a small portion, color red, and keep in a warm place. Pull remaining candy as soon as it can be handled, flavoring with a few drops of oil of peppermint. Pull out into a long strip, and flatten it. Pull the red piece out to the same length, and lay on top. Pull quickly, holding over the stove, or in front of oven, into thin strips, and twist so the strip will be spiral. Keep rolling and twisting until cold, then cut with scissors, or break in short lengths.

Vinegar Candy

2 tbsp butter
2 cups sugar
½ cup vinegar

Put butter in iron kettle or saucepan; when melted, add sugar and vinegar. Stir until sugar is dissolved, wash down crystals from sides of saucepan with butter brush dipped in cold water; boil to 256°F (124.4°C), or until mixture will become brittle when tried in cold water. Turn on buttered platter or marble slab. When cool, pull until very white, and cut in small pieces with scissors or a sharp knife.

CHAPTER VIII

HARD Candies

Brittle candies like butterscotch, barley sugar, peppermint sticks, brittles and nougats, are cooked to 290°F (143.3°C) or up to 330°F (165.5°C).

They should be thin and very brittle when finished.

Candies boiled to a high temperature and pulled must be handled with canvas gloves, in front of a warm oven or batch warmer. Much experience is required to successfully manipulate the syrup used in making Christmas and stick candies, and it will hardly pay the home candy maker to attempt them.

Barley Sugar Drops

2 cups sugar
Color paste
1 cup water
¼ tsp cream of tartar
Flavoring extract

Put sugar and water in saucepan, stir until dissolved, add coloring if desired, cover, and boil 3 minutes. Remove cover, add cream of tartar, and boil to 300°F (148.9°C), or until it just begins to change color. Add few drops of flavoring – peppermint, lemon, or orange extract – and drop at once on tin sheet from tip of spoon, in portions the size of a silver half dollar. Store in a tight glass jar.

Barley Sugar Sticks

Prepare candy as directed in Barley Sugar Drops. Pour on tin sheet in strips four inches long and three fourths inch wide. Take up one at a time, twist, and place in covered glass jars.

Butterscotch I

1⅓ cups brown sugar
⅔ cup butter
2 tsp vinegar
⅔ cup hot water
½ tbsp vanilla

Put sugar, vinegar, butter, and water in saucepan. Stir until ingredients are mixed, bring to boiling point, and boil without stirring to 290°F (143.3°C), or until candy becomes brittle when tried in cold water. Add vanilla, remove from fire, pour into a buttered pan, cool slightly, and mark in squares.

Butterscotch II

½ cup corn syrup
½ cup butter
1⅓ cups sugar
⅔ cup cold water
⅔ cup light brown sugar
½ tbsp vanilla

Put ingredients, except vanilla, in saucepan, and boil to 288°F (142.2°C), or until it cracks when tried in cold water. Add vanilla, turn into buttered tin, cool slightly, and mark in squares.

Scotch Mallows

Dip marshmallows (whole or cut in halves) in Butterscotch I or II, while it is still soft. Take up with two-tined fork, and put on buttered marble slab or tin sheet.

Butterscotch Squares

1⅔ cups light brown sugar
⅔ cup corn syrup
½ cup water
1½ tbsp butter
¼ tsp salt
Oil of lemon

Put sugar, corn syrup, and water in saucepan, stir until sugar is dissolved, bring to boiling point, and boil to 280°F (137.8°C), or until it cracks in cold water.

Add butter and salt, and boil to 290°F (143.3°C), or until it reaches the hard crack when tried in cold water. Remove from fire, flavor with oil of lemon, and pour out between bars on slightly moistened slab, mark in squares, and break up when cold.

Butterscotch Wafers

1⅔ cups sugar
⅓ cup corn syrup
½ cup water
1½ tbsp butter
½ tbsp dark molasses
¼ tsp salt
Few drops oil of lemon

Put sugar, corn syrup, and water in saucepan, stir until dissolved, bring to boiling point, and boil to 270°F (126.6°C), or until it is brittle when tried in cold water. Add butter and molasses, and cook to 280°F (137.7°C), or until it cracks in cold water, stirring to prevent burning. While stirring, move the spoon over every part of the bottom of the kettle. Be careful not to stir in just one spot, thus allowing the candy to burn on the other side of the saucepan. Remove from fire, add salt, flavor with oil of lemon, and drop from tip of spoon on oiled marble slab or tin sheet in wafers the size of a quarter of a dollar.

Cream Butterscotch Balls

1 cup white sugar
⅓ cup butter
½ cup brown sugar
½ cup heavy cream
⅓ cup white corn syrup
1 tsp vanilla or lemon extract

Put all the ingredients, except the flavoring, in a saucepan, stir until mixed, bring to boiling point, and boil until mixture is just stiff enough to keep its shape when a little is dropped into cold water. If it can be lifted from the water and remain in a ball when shaped with the fingers, it is done. Remove from fire, add flavoring, pour into a buttered pan, and when cool, shape into small balls, and roll in confectioners' sugar. The candy when removed from the fire may be dropped from the tip of a spoon on an oiled marble slab or tray, into wafers the size of a quarter of a dollar. These should be loosened with a thin-bladed knife before they have time to get hard.

Cream Butterscotch with Nuts

Follow recipe for making Cream Butterscotch Balls. When candy is removed from fire, add half a cup of walnut or pecan nut meats cut in small pieces, and proceed as in Cream Butterscotch Balls.

Toffee

2 cups light brown sugar
½ cup butter
4 tsp vinegar or the juice of one lemon
½ cup English walnut meats

Heat sugar, butter, and vinegar or lemon juice over a moderate fire, stir till the sugar dissolves, then boil without stirring to 270°F (126.6°C), or until syrup forms a hard ball when tried in cold water. Pour carefully around and over the nuts which have been arranged in rows in buttered or oiled pans. When cold, cut in squares, leaving one nut in the center of each square.

Horehound Candy

½ oz dried horehound
1¾ cups sugar
1 cup water
½ cup corn syrup

Put water and horehound, which may be procured of a druggist in one-ounce packages, in a saucepan and simmer half an hour. Strain through double cheesecloth; there should be half a cup of liquid. To liquid add sugar and corn syrup, and stir until mixture boils. Wash down crystals from sides of saucepan with a butter brush dipped in cold water, and boil to 295°F (126.6°C), or until it is very brittle when tried in cold water. Remove at once from the fire, and pour into buttered pan one fourth inch thick, or pour between candy bars.

As soon as it cools a little, loosen it from the pan, and mark in small squares. Go over the marks with a knife until candy is cold, then break with the hands.

Pack in airtight jar, and keep in a cool place, or wrap in wax paper.

Burnt Almonds

3 cups sugar
1 cup water
1 cup blanched almonds

Put two cups of sugar and half a cup of water in saucepan, stir until dissolved, bring to boiling point, put in the blanched almonds, and stir and boil to 300°F (148.9°C), or until there is a cracking sound, and candy begins to discolor.

Remove almonds from syrup to a buttered cake cooler. Put the remaining cup of sugar and half a cup of water in a clean saucepan, stir, and bring to boiling point; add the almonds, and stir and boil until almonds are well coated with sugar. Again drain on cake cooler, and if coating is not sufficiently thick, repeat the process again.

Almond Nougat

½ lb confectioners' sugar (icing sugar)
¼ lb almonds, blanched and finely chopped

Put sugar in an iron frying pan, place on range, and stir constantly until melted; add almonds, and pour on an oiled marble slab. Fold mixture with a broad-bladed knife as it spreads, keeping it constantly in motion. Divide in four parts, and as soon as cool enough to handle, shape in long rolls about one third inch in diameter, keeping rolls in motion until almost cold. When cold, snap in pieces one and one half inches long. This is done by holding roll at point to be snapped over the sharp edge of a broad-bladed knife and snapping.

These pieces may be dipped in melted confectioners' chocolate.

Nougat Drops

Drop Almond Nougat mixture from the tip of a spoon on an oiled marble slab as soon as taken from fire. These drops have a rough surface. When cold, dip in melted confectioners' chocolate, if desired.

Peanut Nougat

2 cups sugar
1 quart peanuts
¼ tsp salt

Shell, remove skins, and finely chop peanuts. Sprinkle with one fourth teaspoon salt. Put sugar in hot iron frying pan, place on range, and stir constantly with wooden spoon until melted to a syrup, taking care to keep sugar from sides of pan. Add nut meats, pour at once into a warm buttered tin, or on marble slab, and mark in small squares. If sugar is not removed from range as soon as melted, it will quickly burn.

Nut Bar

Cover the bottom of a buttered shallow pan with one and one third cups nut meats (sweet chestnut, English walnuts, or almonds) cut in quarters. Pour over two cups sugar, melted as for Peanut Nougat. Mark in bars.

Nut Brittle

1½ cups shelled nuts
1 cup corn syrup
½ cup water
1 cup sugar
¼ tsp salt
1½ tbsp butter
½ tsp lemon extract

Use peanuts or any other nuts desired, sprinkle with salt, and place in oven to become hot. Put sugar, corn syrup, and water in saucepan, stir until it begins to boil, wash down sides of saucepan with a wet butter brush, and cook to 295°F (146.1°C), or until mixture is very brittle when tried in cold water. Add butter, extract, and nuts, and turn into a buttered pan or tray. As soon as it can be handled, turn the mass over, and pull and stretch it out as thin as possible. Break in irregular pieces. In damp weather keep in covered jar that it may not become sticky.

Nougat

Nut Brittle may be poured out so that it will be three fourths of an inch thick, and the top smoothed with a rolling pin. Before it cools it must be cut in pieces one inch long and three eighths of an inch wide, with a sharp knife. If it gets too cold before it is all cut, the candy may be warmed slightly by holding it over the stove.

Peanut Brittle I

1½ cups sugar
⅔ cup corn syrup
1 cup cold water
1½ cups shelled raw Spanish peanuts
2 tbsp butter
½ tbsp vanilla
¾ tbsp soda
½ tbsp cold water

Put sugar, corn syrup, and two thirds cup cold water in iron kettle, stir until mixture boils, cover, and boil 3 minutes. Remove cover, and boil to 275°F (135°C). Add butter and peanuts, and stir constantly about 10 minutes, or until peanuts are cooked. Add vanilla and soda dissolved in half a tablespoon cold water. Stir until thoroughly mixed, and turn on slightly buttered marble slab or agate tray. Spread as thinly as possible, and lift constantly while cooling, using a spatula, and pull to distribute nuts evenly. Flatten and break in pieces.

Peanut Brittle II

2 tbsp butter
½ cup molasses
1½ cups sugar
½ cup water
½ cup corn syrup
1 cup shelled peanuts
¼ tsp soda

Melt butter in saucepan, add sugar, corn syrup, molasses, and water, and boil until brittle when tried in cold water. Add peanuts and soda, mix thoroughly, pour into buttered pan, and crease in squares.

Coconut Cones

2 cups sugar
½ cup water
Grated rind one fourth orange
Few grains cream of tartar
2 cups chopped coconut
Few grains salt

Put sugar, water, and orange rind in saucepan. Stir until boiling point is reached, then add cream of tartar, and boil without stirring to 290°F (143.3°C), or until it will snap when tried in cold water. Add coconut and salt. Mix thoroughly, shape in small cones, and place on wax paper to dry.

CHAPTER IX

GLACÉS AND Pulled Flowers

When sugar and water are boiled to a high temperature with an acid, as cream of tartar or lemon juice, part of the sugar is changed to glucose, and with careful treatment the syrup will remain clear and become very hard. When swung from a bunch of wires, fine threads fly off which look like spun glass. This is called spun sugar. All kinds of nuts and fruits may be dipped in the syrup while it is hot. On a cold day they harden immediately, and remain dry a long time. In warm, damp weather they become sticky and unsatisfactory. They may be rolled in granulated sugar if the weather changes after they have been made.

Candy baskets and flowers require much experience for perfect results, but much pleasure and many attractive pieces may be attained by experimenting with a syrup boiled to the highest temperature it can reach without burning. It is wise to color the syrup before it boils, as stirring color paste into the mixture after it has cooked is liable to make it sugary.

Candy left over from spun sugar or flowers can be warmed by setting the saucepan on a very heatproof mat on the range, and then can be poured out in a thin sheet on a warm tin, and broken in pieces when brittle.

Glacé Nuts

2 cups sugar
1 cup boiling water
⅓ tsp cream of tartar

Put ingredients in a smooth saucepan, stir, place on range, and heat to boiling point. Wash off sugar which adheres to sides of saucepan with a butter brush dipped in cold water, and boil without stirring to 310°F (154.4°C), or until syrup begins to discolor. Remove saucepan at once from fire, and place in a larger pan of cold water to instantly stop the boiling. Remove from cold water, and place in a saucepan of hot water. Take nuts separately on long pins or steel skewers, or with a small pair of tweezers, dip in syrup to cover, remove from syrup, and place on a tin sheet.

Glacé Fruits

For Glacé Fruits, white grapes, strawberries, sections of oranges or mandarins, kumquats, candied cherries and other candied fruits, dates, and figs may be used.

Separate grapes from the clusters, leaving a short piece of stem on each grape.

Strawberries must be carefully dried, and the hulls left on.

Oranges and mandarins should have the skin carefully pulled off, not cut off, and should be separated into sections without breaking the membrane. Seeds may be removed through a tiny opening made on the inside edge of each piece of fruit.

Cherries are used whole. Candied pineapple and other candied fruits should be cut in pieces.

Prepare syrup as for Glacé Nuts, and dip fruit, one piece at a time, using a small pair of tweezers or a candy dipper, cover each piece completely with syrup, and then lay on a bright tin pan. Glacé Fruits keep but a day, and should be attempted only in cold clear weather.

They are attractive when served in individual paper cases.

Marshmallows Glacé

Brush marshmallows, and dip one at a time in syrup prepared as for Glacé Nuts.

Glacé Marzipan

Cut or shape pieces of almond paste, prepared as for Almond Fruits (page 186), and dip pieces one at a time in syrup prepared as for Glacé Nuts.

Jellies Glacé

Cut in cubes Mint Jelly (see page 138), Apple Paste (see page 136) colored red and flavored with oil of clove, or Orange Pastilles (see page 138). Dip in syrup prepared as for Glacé Nuts.

Taffy Apples

6 small red apples
12 dates
1 cup brown sugar
¼ cup nut meats
½ cup water
6 wooden skewers

Wipe and remove cores from apples, stone dates, chop both dates and nuts, mix, and use to fill cavities in apples. Cook sugar and water until brittle when tried in cold water. Put a skewer in each apple, dip apple in syrup; when covered, remove and cool.

Candy Flowers

2 cups sugar
1 cup water
Color paste
¼ tsp cream of tartar

Put sugar and water in saucepan, add color paste as desired – a small bit of red on the end of a toothpick will be sufficient to make pink roses – cover, and boil 3 minutes. With a clean butter brush dipped in water wash all grains of sugar from sides of saucepan to avoid every tendency of the syrup to become granular. Add cream of tartar, put in thermometer if one is to be used, and boil without stirring to 300°F (148.9°C), or until syrup will instantly crack and become like glass when a little is dropped from tip of spoon into cold water. Another way to tell when syrup is done is to boil it until it begins to change color on one side of saucepan. Pour syrup on to a slightly oiled pan or white agate tray, and place tray on top of saucepan of boiling water, on the stove or in front of a gas oven. As soon as candy can be handled it should be pulled until glossy, keeping it always near the heat of a stove. Return candy to tray, allow it to become softened, detach a small portion, and shape into a closely curled rose petal. Place on a marble slab or tin sheet, away from the heat. Shape a second petal, and fold it around the first petal to form center of rose.

Shape eight rose petals, adding them to the rose center one at a time as they are made, holding them in place at the base with a drop of melted candy. If a petal breaks it may be returned to the tray, softened, and molded again, though the gloss of worked-over candy is not so high. After the desired number of roses are made, the remainder of the candy may be colored dark green, and leaves and calyxes made.

These roses are very effective when placed in a bed of white or green spun sugar and used as a garnish for ices. A variety of shapes, colors, and flowers may be made as the artist becomes accustomed to working with the candy, and learns to keep it just warm and soft enough to handle comfortably.

Candy Baskets

2 cups sugar
1 cup water
Color paste
¼ tsp cream of tartar

Put sugar and water in saucepan, stir until dissolved, add coloring if desired, cover, and boil 3 minutes. Remove cover, add cream of tartar, and boil to 300°F (148.9°C), or until it cracks in cold water. Reduce heat if necessary to keep syrup from burning. Pour on to a buttered pan, and keep in a warm place, either in front of a warm gas-stove oven, or on the back of a range.

Take up a small portion, being careful not to burn the fingers, and pull a moment until glossy, make into a flat, even lozenge, pull out evenly until thin as glass, and shape over a small cup or bowl. Keep in a cool place until wanted for use. Candy must be kept warm while handling, and work must be done rapidly. If candy gets brittle too soon, melt it by setting saucepan over the fire on a very heatproof mat, and use again. Shape handles of strips of pulled candy, and fasten to basket with a drop of melted candy.

Fill candy cups with sherbet or bonbons, and decorate with a spray of candy flowers.

Crystal Cups

2 lb sugar
2 cups boiling water
¼ tsp cream of tartar

Put ingredients in a smooth saucepan. Bring to the boiling point and let boil without stirring until syrup reaches a temperature of 290°F (143.3°C), or until candy cracks when tried in cold water.

Wash off sugar which adheres to sides of saucepan with a butter brush dipped in cold water. Set saucepan in larger saucepan containing cold water to instantly stop cooking; then set in a saucepan of boiling water, that syrup may not cool too rapidly.

Brush over a timbale iron with olive oil and wipe with soft paper. Dip into syrup, taking care that syrup covers iron to only two thirds its depth. Remove from syrup, invert iron, and swing in front of an open window. As soon as cup is formed, take from iron. Cool iron and repeat.

It is well to have two irons, so that one may cool while the other is being used. If a color scheme is to be carried out, the syrup may be colored as desired before boiling.

Arrange cups on a bed of spun sugar, and fill with candies.

Spun Sugar

2 cups sugar
1 cup water
⅛ tsp cream of tartar
Color paste

Put sugar, water, and cream of tartar in saucepan, add color paste if desired, and boil without stirring to 310°F (154.4°C), or until syrup spins a very long thread. Place saucepan immediately into a dish of cold water to stop the boiling, and then set it in hot water. Have ready two parallel, horizontal bars about three feet apart, with paper beneath to protect floor from sugar. Dip sugar spinner, or a bunch of wires in syrup, and wave swiftly back and forth between the bars. Syrup will spin long threads; these should be gathered up from time to time and placed on a cool platter. If syrup gets sugary, place it for a moment on the fire to melt. Spun sugar is used as a garnish around molds of ice cream or glacé fruits and nuts. Spun sugar is easily made in cool weather, but softens very quickly in hot weather. It keeps best if put in a tightly covered box or pail in the refrigerator.

CHAPTER X

CRYSTALLIZED Fruits

Fruits, flowers, and leaves are preserved by means of sugar cooked to the crystal or the soft ball stage. When permeated by syrup they may be kept for a long time. A few recipes are given, and others may be easily formulated with different fruits and petals.

Crystallized Mint Leaves

Wipe fresh mint leaves, remove from stems, and brush each leaf with white of egg, beaten until stiff. Dip in one third cup granulated sugar flavored with five drops oil of spearmint. Place closely together on a cake rack covered with wax paper, and let stand in a slow oven until dry. If the leaves are not thoroughly coated, the process may be repeated.

Crystallized Pears

Take Seckel or Bartlett pears which have not begun to ripen, and pare them, leaving the stems on. Prick in several places, cover with cold water, and add a crystal of burnt Alum for each two pears. Bring to boiling point, and cook gently until they are tender, being careful that they do not go to pieces. Put pears in cold water, changing it several times until pears look clear.

Make syrup by boiling two cups sugar and one cup water for 5 minutes, then cool.

Drain pears, cover with cold syrup, and leave for 24 hours. Drain syrup from pears, add one cup sugar, bring to boiling point, cool, and pour over pears. Again let stand for 24 hours, drain syrup, add one cup sugar, bring to boiling point, and pour over the pears while hot.

Again let stand for 24 hours, drain off syrup, and cook until it spins a long thread. Add pears, let them boil for 1 minute, and return both fruit and syrup to the crock for another 24 hours. Drain syrup, cook to 228°F (108.9°C), add pears, let them boil once, remove from syrup, let fruit dry, and it is ready for use.

Candied Cranberries

½ cup sugar
½ cup cranberries
½ cup water

Select firm, red cranberries, wash, dry, and prick two or three times with needle. Boil sugar and water until it spins a thread, put in cranberries, and cook gently until syrup will jelly when tested from tip of spoon. Remove berries, one at a time, to wax paper, and let stand in the air until well dried. Roll in granulated sugar, and use like candied cherries.

Candied Grapefruit Peel

Wash and wipe three thick skinned grapefruit, and remove the peel in six sections lengthwise of fruit. Soak overnight in one quart of cold water to which is added one tablespoon salt. Drain, put in saucepan, cover with cold water, and bring to boiling point; repeat this process three times, cooking in the last water until peel is soft and tender. Drain, and cut with scissors into thin narrow strips. Weigh the peel. Put an equal weight of sugar into a saucepan, add half a cup of water, bring syrup to boiling point, add the peel, and cook until it is clear. Remove each piece separately, drain, and place on a plate to cool, then roll each piece in confectioners' sugar and spread out to dry. When well dried, store in glass jars.

Candied Orange Peel

Remove the peel in lengthwise sections from four oranges, cover with cold water, bring to the boiling point, and cook slowly until soft and tender. Drain, remove the fibrous inside portion, and with the scissors cut peel in thin narrow strips. In a saucepan put one cup of sugar and half a cup of water, and boil until syrup will spin a thread when allowed to drip from the tip of a spoon. Put strips of orange peel into the syrup, and cook until clear. Remove to plate, let stand until cool, and roll in granulated sugar.

Orange Sugar

Cut sugar
Oranges

Rub the entire surface of blocks of sugar over the rind of oranges that have been washed and wiped dry. Crush the blocks of orange sugar with a rolling pin, and force through a coarse strainer.

Lemon Sugar

Use lemons, and follow directions for making Orange Sugar.

Marrons Glacés

1 lb French chestnuts
1 tsp butter
Cold water
⅓ cup lemon juice
2 cups sugar
2 cups water
1 tsp vanilla

Cut a half-inch gash on flat side of chestnuts, and put in frying pan with butter. Shake over fire until butter is melted. Put in hot oven and let stand 5 minutes. Remove from oven, and with a small knife take off shells and skins. Cover chestnuts with cold water, add lemon juice, and soak overnight. Drain, cover with boiling water, simmer gently until tender, and drain. Put sugar and water in saucepan, stir until sugar is dissolved, boil five minutes, add vanilla and chestnuts, and keep hot without boiling for two hours. Drain syrup from nuts, boil until it spins a long thread, pour over the nuts, and leave overnight. Repeat. Again drain, add one teaspoon corn syrup, and boil to 238°F (114.4°C), or until syrup spins a thread. Add chestnuts, and allow syrup to boil up once over the nuts. Remove from fire, stir gently until syrup begins to grain, and remove chestnuts quickly to buttered tin. Serve in paper cases.

CHAPTER XI

FRUIT AND Gelatines Candies

Many fruits contain large amounts of pectin which causes them to jelly when cooked with sugar and cooled. To others dissolved gelatine must be added to make the mixture stiff enough to hold its shape.

Gelatine candies are not as sweet as other candies, as they become firm with little boiling, and less sugar need be used.

Gelatine should always be soaked in cold water until liquid is absorbed, then dissolved in or over boiling water or hot syrup.

Granulated gelatine is most conveniently measured, but sheet or shredded gelatine may be substituted; six sheets of gelatine will take the place of four tablespoons granulated gelatine.

Marshmallows, when made in large quantities, usually contain gum arabic. They are beaten by machinery for a long time, and can be made firmer and lighter than is possible when made by hand.

Therefore, for some purposes, commercial marshmallows will be more satisfactory than those made at home, though a delicate marshmallow can be made, and a variety of colors, shapes, and flavors can be secured with gelatine and egg whites. Gumdrops may be made with gum arabic or with gelatine, and in a variety of flavors, colors, and shapes.

Apricot Paste

1 can apricots
Sugar

Drain syrup from a can of apricots, and rub fruit through a sieve. Measure syrup, and add three fourths as much sugar, put in saucepan, and boil to 254°F (123.3°C), or until syrup cracks when tried in cold water, being careful that it does not burn. Add apricot pulp, and boil, stirring gently to prevent burning, until mixture is so thick that it follows the spoon in stirring, and detaches itself from the saucepan. Pour into a buttered pan, spread in a layer one eighth of an inch thick, and when stiff remove from pan, cut in fancy shapes with small tin cutters, and sprinkle with coarse sugar, or crystallize according to directions on page 140.

Instead of pouring into buttered pan, paste may be dropped on waxed paper in rounds one and one half inches in diameter. These may be dipped in melted chocolate or melted fondant if desired.

Greengage Paste

6 greengage plums
¾ cup sugar
¾ tsp gelatine
1 tbsp cold water
¾ cup syrup from canned greengage plums

Put gelatine in cold water, and leave until it is needed. Drain syrup from canned greengage plums, and rub six plums through a sieve. Put syrup, fruit pulp, and sugar in saucepan, and boil, stirring gently to prevent burning, until mixture drops like thick jelly from the spoon, and holds its shape when tried on a cold saucer. Add soaked gelatine, and when dissolved, pour mixture into a buttered pan, in a layer one eighth of an inch thick. When stiff remove from pan, cut into fancy shapes with small tin cutters, and roll in coarse sugar, or crystallize according to directions on page 140. These may be dipped in melted chocolate or melted fondant if desired.

Apple Paste Candy

5 apples
2 cups water
1½ cups sugar
Flavor

Wipe apples, and cut in pieces, put in saucepan, add water, and cook until apples are soft.

Drain the liquid, of which there should be three fourths cup, into a clean saucepan, add sugar, and boil to 238°F (114.4°C), or until it will form a soft ball when tried in cold water. Rub apple pulp through sieve, add to syrup, and boil, stirring constantly to prevent burning, until mixture is so thick that it leaves the pan, and follows the spoon during the stirring. Add flavor as desired. Orange, raspberry, or lemon extract, one tablespoon lime juice, or a few drops of oil of peppermint are good. Paste may be colored delicately to correspond with flavor used. Drop paste from tip of spoon in rounds on wax paper, or spread in a buttered pan, let it dry, and cut in fancy shapes. Roll in coarse sugar or crystallize.

Apricot Marshmallows

Prepare Apricot Paste. Cut marshmallows in two pieces crosswise, or cut circles one inch in diameter from a sheet of marshmallow. Dip marshmallows one at a time in the fruit paste before it stiffens, and place on wax paper. When all are dipped, roll in granulated sugar.

This paste may be used as filling for dates, or as a center for chocolates, or for coating pieces of marshmallow paste.

Greengage Marshmallows

Prepare Greengage Paste as in recipe, and proceed as in recipe for Apricot Marshmallows.

Fruit Marshmallows

Prepare Apple Paste as in recipe, flavor with lime and color green. Proceed as in recipe for Apricot Marshmallows.

Apricot Marshmallow Squares

Prepare Apricot Paste, and pour half of it one fourth inch deep in a square pan which has been rinsed in cold water and not dried, or between candy bars. Cover with a piece of sheet marshmallow the same size as the pan, and pour remaining paste over the marshmallow. When firm, cut in squares and roll in granulated sugar.

Greengage Marshmallow Squares

Prepare Greengage Paste, and proceed as in Apricot Marshmallow Squares.

Fruit Marshmallow Squares

Prepare Apple Paste, and proceed as in Apricot Marshmallow Squares.

Mint Jelly Bonbons

6 apples
2 cups water
¾ cup sugar
2 tbsp gelatine
4 tbsp cold water
Few drops oil of peppermint
Green color paste

Wipe apples, and cut in quarters, add two cups cold water, and cook until very soft. Drain through cheesecloth; there should be one cup of juice. Put in saucepan and boil 10 minutes; add sugar, boil 5 minutes, add gelatine which has been soaked in four tablespoons cold water, stir until gelatine is dissolved, and remove from fire. Flavor with two or three drops of oil of peppermint, color green, and pour into a bread pan. When firm, cut in small cubes, and roll in granulated sugar, or dip in melted coating chocolate.

Orange Pastilles

1⅙ cups confectioners' sugar (icing sugar)
6 tbsp cold water
½ tbsp corn syrup
1 tbsp gelatine
2 tbsp orange juice
Orange color paste

Put half a cup of confectioners' sugar and two tablespoons cold water in saucepan; when dissolved, add corn syrup, bring to boiling point, then add gelatine soaked in four tablespoons cold water, the orange juice, and orange color paste to color delicately. Sift the remaining sugar on a platter, pour mixture into the center, and allow it to cool. Then work with a broad spatula until it begins to get thick and smooth. Pat and spread into a layer one inch thick, allow it to harden, then cut into squares, and roll in orange sugar.

Gumdrops 1

6½ level tbsp granulated gelatine
1 tbsp water
1⅓ cups sugar
½ cup corn syrup
1⅓ cups cold water
3 tbsp lemon juice

Soak gelatine in one and one fourth cups water until liquid is absorbed. Put sugar, corn syrup, and one tablespoon water in saucepan, stir until mixed, bring to boiling point, and boil without stirring to 240°F (115.5°C), or until mixture forms a soft ball when tried in cold water. Add gelatine, stir over fire 1 minute, add lemon juice, strain, and let stand 5 minutes in a cool place. Mold in cornstarch as directed on page 82. Impressions the size and shape of a gumdrop can be made with the round end of the handle of a vegetable knife. When firm, place in sifter, and shake and brush off superfluous starch or flour. Crystallize as directed in following recipe, or hold a moment in the steam from a tea kettle, and roll in coarse granulated sugar.

One teaspoon raspberry extract and pink color paste, or four teaspoons orange extract and orange color paste, or a few drops oil of lime and green color paste, may be added when mixture is removed from the fire, to give a variety of gumdrops.

To Crystallize Candies

4 cups sugar
2 cups water
Gumdrops or bonbons

Put sugar and water in saucepan, stir until dissolved, and boil without stirring to 224°F (106.7°C), or until syrup forms a very soft ball that will not hold its shape when tried in cold water.

Remove from fire and set saucepan in a dish of cold water, cover with a damp cloth, and let stand until lukewarm. Do not disturb the syrup in any way, as it very easily becomes sugary. Place candies that are to be crystallized in shallow cake pans, gently pour on syrup until the candies are covered, cover pan with a tin cover, and set away to crystallize for 10 or 12 hours, or until crystals are visible all over the candies. Tip the pans until the syrup runs out. Leave the candies until dry, then pack in wax paper.

When large amounts of candy are to be crystallized, it is well to use a syrup gauge. Syrup should be tested at a temperature of 60°F (14.5°C), and should register from 32½° to 35° on the Baumé scale.

Gumdrops II

½ lb powdered gum arabic
1 cup hot water
2¼ cups sugar
1 cup cold water
Color
Flavor

Put gum arabic and hot water in double boiler, keep over hot water until dissolved, then strain. Put sugar and cold water in saucepan, stir until sugar is dissolved, wash down sides of saucepan with a butter brush dipped in cold water, and boil to 270°F (132.2°C), or until mixture cracks when tried in cold water. Set saucepan at once over hot water, add dissolved gum arabic, and leave 30 minutes. Color and flavor as desired, skim, run into starch molds, cover with starch, and leave 2 days. Brush off starch and crystallize, or hold a moment in steam from a tea kettle, and roll in coarse granulated sugar. The inside of these gumdrops should be a thick syrup.

Suggestions for Color and Flavor for Gumdrops

Leave uncolored, use lemon extract or lemon juice
Leave uncolored, use peppermint flavor
Leave uncolored, use liquorice extract.
Color orange, use orange extract.
Color yellow, use oil of sassafras
Color green, use oil of lime
Color red, use oil of clove
Color pink, use raspberry extract
Color pink, use rose flavor
Color pink, use wintergreen flavor

Suggestions for Shapes for Gumdrops

Small cones
Medium cones
Large cones
Bars
Circles
Rings
Cubes

Orange Gumdrops

6½ tbsp gelatine
1 cup water
½ cup orange juice (strained)
1¾ cups sugar
½ cup corn syrup
1 tbsp water
Grated rind ½ orange

Soak gelatine in orange juice and one cup water until liquid is absorbed. Cook sugar, corn syrup, orange rind, and 1 tablespoon water to 240°F (115.5°C), or until a soft ball is formed when mixture is tried in cold water. Add gelatine, stir 1 minute, remove from fire, and strain. Let stand 5 minutes, remove scum, and pour into starch molds. When firm, place in sifter, and shake or brush off superfluous starch. Crystallize as directed on page 140, or hold a moment in the steam from a tea kettle, and roll in coarse granulated sugar. Raspberry or other fruit juice may be used in place of orange juice and rind.

Turkish Delight

1 oz sheet gelatine
½ cup cold water
2 cups sugar
½ cup boiling water
⅓ cup orange juice
3 tbsp lemon juice
Grated rind one orange
Red color paste

Break gelatine in pieces, add cold water, cover, and let soak 2 hours. Put sugar and boiling water in saucepan, stir until it boils, add gelatine, stir until gelatine is dissolved and occasionally while candy simmers, for 20 minutes. Add fruit juices, orange rind, and coloring if desired. Rinse a small bread pan with cold water, and pour in mixture one inch deep. Let stand until cold, remove to board, cut in cubes, and roll in confectioners' sugar.

Marshmallows

2 cups sugar
½ cup corn syrup
½ cup hot water
4 tbsp gelatine
4 tbsp cold water
2 small egg whites
1 tsp vanilla
1 tbsp cornstarch

Put sugar, corn syrup, and hot water in saucepan, and stir until sugar is dissolved, bring to boiling point and boil without stirring to 240°F (115.5°C), or until it forms a soft ball when tried in cold water. Remove from fire, add gelatine which has soaked in the cold water, and beat mixture until it is white. Add whites of eggs beaten until stiff, and beat candy vigorously until it gets thick and stringy. Add vanilla and cornstarch, pour into a pan nine inches square that has been with dusted over with sifted confectioners' sugar, and sift confectioners' sugar over the top of the candy in the pan. Cut into squares with a silver knife that is kept moist by being dipped into water. Let candy stand overnight to dry off, then pack between layers of wax paper. Other flavors, and nuts or candied fruits cut in small pieces, may be added if desired.

Walnut Marshmallows

To above recipe for Marshmallows add half a cup of finely chopped walnut meats with vanilla and cornstarch. These may be dipped in melted coating chocolate if desired.

Toasted Marshmallows I

Put a marshmallow on the end of a long skewer, hatpin, or sharp pointed stick, and hold over a bed of glowing coals in the fireplace or out of doors, turning the marshmallows over and over, until golden brown on the outside and soft inside. Eat at once.

Toasted Marshmallows II

Put marshmallows in a strainer, and dip quickly in and out of a kettle of water at a temperature of about 100°F (37.7°C). Drain and put on marble slab covered with roasted coconut. Mix thoroughly until each marshmallow is completely coated.

To Roast Coconut

Sprinkle shredded coconut on a tin baking sheet, put in the oven, stirring occasionally, and roast until a delicate brown.

Gelatine Nougat

1 cup water
4 tbsp gelatine
1 cup sugar
1 tsp corn syrup
1 egg white
1 tsp almond extract
½ cup blanched almonds
⅓ cup candied cherries
⅓ cup pistachio nuts

Put gelatine in saucepan, add cold water, and let stand 5 minutes. Add sugar and corn syrup, put over fire, and stir constantly until mixture has boiled 8 minutes. Beat the egg white until stiff, add syrup slowly while beating, and then add remaining ingredients.

Mix one tablespoon each of cornstarch and confectioners' sugar, and sprinkle in a bread pan. Pour in mixture, and when quite firm cut in bars and wrap in wax paper.

Wintergreen Wafers

1 tsp gelatine
2 tsp cold water
3 tsp boiling water
Few drops oil of wintergreen
Confectioners' sugar (icing sugar)

Soak gelatine in cold water 5 minutes, dissolve in boiling water, and strain through a fine wire strainer. Add oil of wintergreen, and gradually stir in sifted confectioners' sugar until mixture is stiff enough to knead. Put candy on a board or marble slab dredged with confectioners' sugar, and knead until smooth, then roll as thin as cardboard, and cut out in discs or fancy shapes. For children's parties the initial of the first name of each child may be cut out of the thinly rolled candy. With fancy cutters or a model cut from cardboard, birds and animals may be cut out, and used for favors.

Assorted Wafers

Prepare mixture as for Wintergreen Wafers, omitting the oil of wintergreen. Substitute the following combinations of color and flavor, dividing the mixture into several portions, and coloring and flavoring each portion differently. Finish like Wintergreen Wafers.

With oil of clove use scarlet color paste
With oil of cinnamon use rose color paste
With oil of lime use green color paste
With orange extract use orange color paste
With lemon extract use yellow color paste
With melted chocolate use vanilla extract

Orange Wafers

Peel of 2 oranges
¾ cup orange juice
¼ cup water
1 cup sugar
3 tbsp gelatine
1 tsp orange extract

Soak orange peel in cold water to cover overnight, then boil 1 hour, changing the water every 15 minutes. Drain, and grind the peel to a pulp, then add sugar, half a cup of orange juice, and one fourth cup water, and boil, stirring occasionally to prevent burning, until thick and syrupy. Add gelatine soaked in remaining one fourth cup orange juice, mix well, add orange extract, and drop from tip of teaspoon on to a buttered marble slab or oiled paper. Before wafers have time to stiffen, place a nut meat in center. A small amount of mixture can be combined with finely chopped pecan nut meats and candied cherries, and used as a filling between two wafers. Wafers can be dipped in melted coating chocolate if desired.

CHAPTER
XII

DRIED FRUIT
and
Nuts

Dried fruits are rich in sugar, which is the reason that they can be kept for a long time.

Some of them need little preparation to make them take the place of candy.

Nuts furnish the foodstuffs in which fruits are deficient. When fruits and nuts are combined, very nutritious candies are obtained. A few combinations are given in this chapter, and others can be made as fancy and circumstances dictate.

A study of the food values will show what an important place these combinations may hold in the diet, even taking the place on a tramp or a railroad journey of bread and meat. A basket of salted nuts and stuffed fruits makes a gift that is always appreciated.

To Blanch Almonds

Cover shelled almonds with boiling water, let stand 2 minutes, drain, cover with cold water, again drain. Brown skins can be easily slipped off with the fingers. Dry the nuts on a towel or piece of cheesecloth. Pistachio nuts and English walnuts may be blanched in the same way.

Salted Mixed Nuts

Beat the white of one egg slightly, add nut meats of many kinds, and stir until they are entirely covered with the egg. Remove nuts from the egg and put in a dripping pan, sprinkle with salt and bake in a hot oven until nuts are heated through. Keep oven door open while baking, and stir nuts often, that they may not burn.

Salted Almonds

1 cup Jordan almonds
½ cup olive or cooking oil
Salt

Cover almonds with boiling water, let stand 2 minutes, drain, cover with cold water, again drain, and remove brown skins. Dry on a towel. Heat oil in very small frying pan; when hot, put in enough almonds to cover bottom of pan, and stir until delicately browned. Remove with spoon or small skimmer, taking up as little oil as possible. Drain on brown paper, and sprinkle with salt. Repeat, until all are fried. Cottonseed oil, peanut oil, or half lard and half clarified butter may be used instead of olive oil.

Salted Peanuts

1 cup raw peanuts
½ cup cooking oil

Remove skins from peanuts and fry same as salted almonds.

Salted Pecans

1 cup pecan nut meats
½ cup cooking oil

Use whole nut meats and fry same as Salted Almonds. Be careful that they do not remain in the fat too long. As they are dark, the color does not show when they are sufficiently cooked.

Spiced Nuts

Prepare salted nuts, and when sprinkling with salt sprinkle also with powdered clove, powdered cinnamon, or a mixture of spices. Popcorn may be prepared in the same way. Use instead of salted nuts.

How to Color Almonds

Blanch and chop almonds, spread on white paper, and add a few drops of color. Rub together until pieces are all colored alike, then dry carefully, and keep in covered glass jar. Green chopped almonds may be used instead of pistachio nuts, if the latter are not obtainable.

Sugared Peanuts

1 cup shelled roasted peanuts
1 cup sugar
½ cup water
½ tsp vanilla

Remove brown skins from peanuts, put nuts in a saucepan, and keep in a warm place. Put sugar and water in another saucepan, stir until sugar is dissolved, and boil without stirring to 238°F (114.4°C), or until candy forms a soft ball when tried in cold water. Hold pan of peanuts several inches above the fire and shake vigorously while slowly pouring syrup over the nuts. Occasionally stir the nuts, then add remaining syrup drop by drop until all is used. Nuts should be evenly covered with a coating of sugar. If coating is not thick enough, more sugar and water may be boiled and added as before.

Sugared Almonds

1 cup shelled almonds
1 cup sugar
½ cup water
½ tsp vanilla

Proceed as in making Sugared Peanuts, blanching the almonds or not, as preferred.

Stuffed Dates

Wash and stone as many dates as are needed and stuff with any of the following:

English walnut meats, broken in pieces
Pecan nut meats, broken in pieces
Salted peanuts, chopped
Peanut butter
Candied ginger, cut fine
Candied pineapple, cut fine
Roasted almonds
Brazil nuts, brown skin removed

After stuffing, roll the dates in granulated or confectioners' sugar, and arrange on a doily, or pack in layers in a box between wax paper.

Fried Stuffed Dates

¾ lb dates
2 tbsp butter
1 cup coconut
½ cup chopped nuts
½ tsp vanilla

Wash and dry dates, remove stones, and sauté in butter on both sides. Stuff dates with chopped nuts flavored with vanilla, and roll dates in shredded coconut. Wrap in wax paper and twist the ends, or pack in layers in a box lined with wax paper.

Stuffed Figs I

16 figs
8 maraschino cherries
16 pecan nut meats
Granulated sugar

Use figs that come in boxes, baskets, or in glass jars. Wash them, dry on cheesecloth, make an opening in each, and stuff with half a maraschino cherry, and one nut meat broken in pieces. Roll in granulated sugar, and put in paper cases.

Stuffed Figs II

16 figs
½ cup salted almonds
Granulated sugar

Use figs that come in boxes, baskets, or in glass jars. Wash them, dry on cheesecloth, make an opening in each, and stuff with salted almonds finely chopped. Roll in granulated sugar, and put in paper cases.

Stuffed Figs III

16 figs
8 marshmallows
16 walnut meats
Granulated sugar

Use figs that come in bags, baskets, or glass jars, rather than pressed figs; wash and dry them, make an opening in each, stuff with half a marshmallow and a chopped walnut cut fine. Roll in granulated sugar, and place in paper cases.

Stuffed Prunes

1 lb selected prunes
Confectioners' sugar (icing sugar)

Selected prunes may be purchased in glass jars, with from twenty-eight to forty-five prunes in a pound. Remove stones, stuff half the prunes, each with another prune, and roll in confectioners' sugar. If preferred, fondant or chopped salted nuts may be used for stuffing.

Raisin Clusters

Take a large bunch of raisins, and without removing them from the stem, slit each raisin, remove seeds, and put in opening a tiny ball of fondant – white, pink, or green – flavored with vanilla, rose, or almond.

Tie with a ribbon. Use to garnish a loaf of fruit cake or top of box of candy.

Stuffed Cluster Raisins

Steam stem raisins, leaving them in small clusters. When soft, make a tiny cut with a sharp pointed knife at the end opposite the stem, and remove the seeds. Blanch Jordan almonds, cook in hot olive oil until delicately browned, sprinkle sparingly with salt, and insert an almond in each raisin, letting it protrude from the end.

Quick Fruit Cake

¾ cup raisins
¼ cup walnut meats
Few grains salt

Wash raisins, dry them, and put through a meat grinder with the nuts. Mix well, season with salt, shape in small cakes, and wrap in paraffin paper. These are excellent on a picnic, or to keep on hand in the automobile when refreshment is wanted during an emergency. They may be sent to soldiers on duty, as they contain concentrated nourishment, and will keep indefinitely without spoiling.

Fruit Nut Caramels

1 cup figs
2 cups walnuts
1 cup dates

Wash and stone the dates, wash figs, and remove stems, and put with the nuts through meat grinder. Mix together thoroughly, and press firmly three fourths inch thick into a small buttered pan. Cut in squares and wrap in wax paper, or shape in small balls and roll in confectioners' sugar.

Chocolate Circles

½ cup walnuts
½ cup figs
½ cup almond paste
Grated rind one orange
¼ tsp salt
2 squares unsweetened chocolate
Orange juice
Sugar
Blanched almonds

Put walnuts, figs, and almond paste through meat grinder, add orange rind, salt and enough orange juice to make mixture of consistency to handle.

Knead on a board or marble slab sprinkled with sugar, cut in circles, brush with chocolate melted over hot water, and decorate with pieces of almonds.

Date and Nut Butter

1 cup dates
1¼ cups shelled peanuts
Few grains salt
4 tbsp cream

Remove stones from dates, and put dates and peanuts twice through meat grinder, using nut butter cutter. Mix thoroughly with salt, and pack in glass jars. When wanted for use add cream, and work with a spatula until the consistency of butter. Use in candies in place of peanut butter, or use as a sandwich filling.

Peanut Butter

Use roasted peanuts, which may be purchased by the pound ready shelled. Remove brown skins, and put twice through the meat grinder, using nut butter disc. Add half a teaspoon of salt to each pound of nut meats. When wanted for use add heavy cream or butter, mixing thoroughly.

MERINGUES and Macaroons

Mixtures of white of egg and sugar, with or without chopped nuts, when baked in the oven, are a cross between cakes and candies. To secure the best results, materials should be carefully combined and slowly baked.

Almonds shelled, blanched, and finely ground are the chief ingredient of almond paste. This can be made at home, or can be purchased ready for use in one pound, five pound, and larger packages, at about the same cost. It is the basis of a large variety of macaroons, and is also used for marzipan fruits, flowers, and vegetables.

Meringues or Kisses

4 egg whites
1 cup fine granulated sugar
½ tsp vanilla

Beat whites of eggs until stiff and add, a spoonful at a time, two thirds cup sugar, beating vigorously between each addition, and continue to beat until mixture will hold its shape. Carefully cut and fold in vanilla and remaining sugar. Drop from tip of spoon, or force through pastry bag and tube on tin sheet or wet board covered with a sheet of paper. Bake 30 minutes in a very slow oven, not allowing them to change color until the last few minutes, when they should become a very delicate brown. Remove from oven, invert paper and kisses, and wet paper with a damp cloth, when kisses may be easily removed.

French Meringues

2 cups sugar
⅔ cup water
5 egg whites
1 tsp vanilla

Put sugar and water in saucepan, stir until dissolved, and boil to 242°F (116.7°C), or until a firm ball is formed when tried in cold water. When syrup is ready, beat whites of eggs until stiff, and add syrup slowly, continuing the beating. Set dish containing mixture in saucepan of cold water, add vanilla, and fold over and over for 5 minutes. Cover and let stand for 15 minutes. Shape with a spoon or pastry bag and tube on a buttered sheet dredged with cornstarch. Sprinkle with pink or yellow sugar, and bake 30 minutes in so slow an oven that the sugar does not discolor. Hearts, wreaths, stars, and roses are attractive shapes.

Mushroom Meringues

Force meringue mixture through pastry bag and plain tube in rounds one and one half inches in diameter, for mushroom caps. Shape stems three fourths inch in diameter and one to one and one half inches high.

Sprinkle all with grated chocolate or cocoa, rubbing it gently on with the finger. Bake in a slow oven, remove paper, and place caps on stems.

Turkey Meringues

Shape meringue mixture on paper with pastry bag and rose tube in the shape of turkeys. Shape the spread tail first on the paper, in front of tail shape the body, building it up in circles and shaping the head last.

Bake, remove from paper, and scoop out soft part, dry in oven, fill with ice cream, stand in a nest of green spun sugar, and serve.

Nut Meringues

To either recipe for Meringues add half a cup of chopped nut meats of any kind, and one fourth teaspoon of salt. Drop from tip of spoon, or force through pastry bag and plain tube, on tin sheet covered with a sheet of paper. Sprinkle with nut meats, and bake like meringues.

Coconut Meringues

2 egg whites
½ cup fine granulated sugar
½ tsp vanilla
Few grains salt
½ cup coconut shredded

Beat whites of eggs until very stiff, add slowly vanilla and one fourth cup sugar, continuing the beating. Fold in remaining sugar, salt, and coconut. Shape with spoon or with pastry bag and tube on tin sheet covered with paper, and bake 30 minutes in slow oven.

Praline Kisses

¾ cup almonds
2 tbsp water
¼ cup sugar
2 egg whites
⅔ cup confectioners' sugar (icing sugar)
¼ tsp vanilla
1 tsp salt

Blanch almonds, finely shred three eighths cup, and dry slowly in the oven. Put water and sugar in small omelet pan, stir until it boils, add remaining almonds, and cook until the syrup is golden brown. Turn into a pan, cool, and force through grinder. Beat whites of eggs until stiff, add confectioners' sugar slowly, continuing the beating, then fold in shredded and ground almonds, vanilla, and salt. Shape in cones on a tin sheet covered with paper. Sift sugar over them, and bake in slow oven 25 minutes.

Coconut Cakes

1 fresh coconut
2 tbsp corn syrup
7 tbsp sugar
1 egg white

Grate sufficient fresh coconut to make two cups. This will take about half a coconut.

Put with corn syrup and sugar in top of double boiler, and stir and cook until mixture clings to spoon. Add white of egg, and cook until mixture feels sticky when tried between the fingers. Spread in a wet pan, cover with wet paper, and cool; then chill by setting pan on ice in the refrigerator. Shape into balls, first dipping the hands in cold water. If one and one half tablespoons of mixture are used for each, ten cakes can be made. Heat a tin sheet slightly, and rub over with white wax, paraffin, or olive oil. Place balls on the sheet, and bake in a slow oven about 20 minutes.

Cornettes

Popped corn
1 egg white
⅓ cup sugar
¾ tbsp butter
¼ tsp salt
½ tsp vanilla
Candied cherries
Chopped almonds

Chop sufficient popped corn to make three fourths cup. Beat white of egg until stiff, and add gradually sugar, butter – softened but not melted – salt, and vanilla. Fold in popped corn, drop from teaspoon on buttered sheet, and shape in circular forms with a fork dipped in cold water. Place a piece of candied cherry in the center of each, sprinkle with finely chopped almonds, and bake in a slow oven until delicately browned.

Baked Peanut Candy

1 quart peanuts
1 egg white
1 cup brown sugar
¼ tsp salt
½ tsp vanilla

Shell one quart peanuts or use one cup shelled peanuts; remove skins, and put through coarse meat grinder. Beat white of egg until light; add slowly while beating constantly brown sugar, salt, and vanilla.

Fold in the ground peanuts, drop from tip of spoon on buttered tin sheet, and bake in a slow oven.

Date and Almond Meringues

¾ cup Jordan almonds
½ cup dates
2 egg whites
⅔ cup confectioners' sugar (icing sugar)
½ tsp vanilla
¼ tsp salt
1 tsp lemon juice

Blanch the almonds, wash dates, and remove stones, and put both almonds and dates through meat chopper together. Beat whites of eggs until stiff, then add gradually, while beating constantly, one third cup sugar, the vanilla, salt, and lemon juice, and fold into the mixture the nuts, dates, and one fourth cup sugar. Drop from tip of spoon on buttered tin sheet one inch apart. Sprinkle with confectioners' sugar, and bake in a moderate oven from 12 to 15 minutes.

Cinnamon Circles

1½ cups almonds
2 egg whites
1 cup powdered sugar
⅓ grated lemon rind
1 tsp cinnamon
1 cup confectioners' sugar (icing sugar)
Water
½ tsp vanilla

Chop almonds without blanching. Beat whites of eggs until stiff, add gradually the powdered sugar mixed with lemon rind and cinnamon, and fold in the almonds. Dredge a board or marble slab with flour and then with powdered sugar, turn out mixture, pat with rolling pin, and roll to one fourth inch in thickness. Shape with a small round cutter, place on a slightly buttered tin sheet, and bake in a moderate oven. Cover with frosting made of confectioners' sugar, vanilla, and enough water to make of the right consistency to spread.

Almond Paste

½ lb blanched almonds
1 lb confectioners' sugar (icing sugar)
2 egg yolks
Rose water
Almond extract

Dry almonds and put through the meat chopper, using a fine grinding knife. Add confectioners' sugar, and melt slightly over the fire, add yolks of eggs beaten until thick and lemon colored, and cook until mixture is thick enough to spread.

Mix rose water and almond extract in equal portions, and use to flavor the paste to taste.

Use additional rose water to make it the right consistency, working it on a slab with a spatula.

For macaroons it should be a stiff mixture; for shaping into flowers, fruits, etc, it may be a little softer.

Macaroons

½ lb almond paste
1 cup sugar (scant)
4 egg whites
⅓ cup confectioners' sugar (icing sugar)

Break almond paste into small pieces, and mix with the hand, adding gradually the one scant cup of sugar and the whites of eggs, of which there should be a scant half cup. When perfectly blended, stir in the confectioners' sugar.

Shape with pastry bag and tube on tin sheets covered with thin paper, and bake in a slow oven. Remove from oven, invert paper and macaroons, and wet paper with a cloth wrung out of cold water, when macaroons may be easily removed.

Christmas Macaroons

Frost macaroons with ornamental frosting, and decorate with a wreath of green frosting leaves tied with a red bow of frosting.

Almond Macaroons

Prepare macaroons as in recipe above, and before baking, sprinkle with almonds blanched, and shredded or chopped.

Almond Cakes

½ lb almond paste
½ cup confectioners' sugar (icing sugar)
Egg white
Blanched almonds

Put almond paste and confectioners' sugar through a puree strainer, and work with spatula until well blended. Add just enough unbeaten white of egg to make mixture of such a consistency that it may be easily formed into balls. Roll each ball in slightly beaten white of egg, press two balls together for each cake, and where balls are joined insert in each ball half a blanched almond. Bake in a very slow oven.

Scrolls

½ lb almond paste
½ cup confectioners' sugar (icing sugar)
1 small egg white
Chopped nuts

Work almond paste and sugar together on marble slab, add egg gradually, working it in with a spatula until mixture is perfectly smooth. Shape mixture, which should be quite soft, in a long roll. Cut off pieces three inches long, roll in nuts, shape like a scroll, and lay on a buttered tin sheet. Bake 20 minutes in a slow oven, and frost with confectioners' sugar mixed with two tablespoons water and one teaspoon lemon juice.

True Lovers' Knots

Put Scroll Mixture into bag with small tube in the end, and shape on buttered sheet like bow knots. Sprinkle with chopped nuts. Bake 20 minutes in a slow oven.

Cornflake Macaroons

2 egg whites
1 cup sugar
½ cup shredded coconut
⅓ tsp salt
2 cups cornflakes

Beat whites of eggs until stiff, and add gradually the sugar and salt; then fold in the cornflakes and coconut. Drop mixture from tip of teaspoon on a well-greased tin sheet one inch apart. Bake in a moderate oven until delicately browned. Remove from pan while warm.

Chocolate Almond Macaroons

2 egg whites
¾ cup confectioners' sugar (icing sugar)
1 oz unsweetened chocolate
½ cup Jordan almonds

Beat eggs until stiff, and add sugar gradually, while beating constantly. Carefully cut and fold in chocolate which has been melted and slightly cooled, and two thirds of the nut meats blanched and chopped. Drop mixture from tip of teaspoon on buttered tin sheet, sprinkle with remaining nuts, and bake in a slow oven.

Peanut Macaroons

2 egg whites
½ cup fine granulated sugar
1 tsp vanilla
⅔ cup shelled peanuts

Beat whites of eggs until stiff, and add sugar and vanilla gradually, continuing the beating. Finely chop peanuts, and fold them into the egg mixture. Drop from tip of spoon on buttered and floured tin sheet, one and one half inches apart. Place half a peanut on each macaroon, and bake in a slow oven 12 to 15 minutes.

Pecan Macaroons

1 egg white
1 cup brown sugar
1 cup pecan nut meats
¼ tsp salt

Beat white of egg until stiff, add sugar gradually, continuing the beating. Fold in nut meats, finely chopped and sprinkled with salt. Drop from tip of spoon, one inch apart, on a buttered and floured sheet, and bake in a moderate oven about 12 minutes, or until delicately browned.

POPCORN

Candies

How to Pop Corn

Put about half a cup of corn in popper, and shake over a moderate fire until kernels begin to pop. If gas is used, turn it very low, that corn may become uniformly heated through. Shake rapidly as soon as kernels begin to pop, and remove from fire before they begin to burn.

Half a cup of popcorn should yield one and one half quarts popped corn. For salted popped corn, sprinkle generously with salt.

Buttered Popcorn

4 tbsp butter
2 quarts popped corn
Salt

Melt butter in large saucepan, add corn, and stir until every kernel is coated. Sprinkle with salt and serve at once.

Corn Balls

5 quarts popped corn
2 cups sugar
½ cup white corn syrup
1½ cups water
⅓ tsp salt
1 tsp vinegar
1 tbsp vanilla

Carefully pick over the corn, discarding all that is not tender, and put perfect kernels into a large pan. Put sugar, corn syrup, and water in saucepan, stir until well mixed, bring to boiling point, and boil without stirring to 260°F (126.7°C), or until it cracks when tried in cold water. Add vinegar and vanilla, and boil to 264°F (128.9°C). Remove from fire, and pour slowly over the corn, stirring and turning over the corn with a spoon, so that every kernel will be evenly coated with syrup.

Make sugared corn into balls, and wrap in wax paper.

Molasses Corn Balls

3 quarts popped corn
1 cup molasses
½ cup sugar
1 tbsp butter
½ tsp salt

Pick over popped corn, discarding all hard kernels, put in a large pan, and sprinkle with salt.

Melt butter in saucepan, add molasses and sugar, and boil to 270°F (132.2°C), or until candy is brittle when tried in cold water. Pour mixture slowly over the corn, stirring constantly. Shape into balls, using as little pressure as possible. Wrap in wax paper.

Maple Corn Balls

3 quarts popped corn
½ cup sugar
1 cup maple syrup
1 tbsp butter
1 tsp salt

Pop corn and pick over, discarding kernels that do not pop, and put in large kettle. Melt butter in saucepan, and add syrup and sugar. Bring to the boiling point, and let boil until mixture will become brittle when tried in cold water. Pour mixture gradually, while stirring constantly, over corn which has been sprinkled with salt. Shape into balls, using as little pressure as possible.

Popcorn Nuggets

2 cups sugar
⅔ cup water
¼ tsp cream of tartar
⅓ cup dark molasses
2 tbsp butter
Few grains salt
5 quarts popcorn

Put sugar, water, and cream of tartar in saucepan, bring to boiling point, and boil without stirring to 280°F (137.8°C), or until syrup will crack when tried in cold water. Remove thermometer, add molasses, butter, and salt, and boil, stirring constantly, until candy will become very brittle when tried in cold water, being careful that it does not burn. Have ready a pan containing popped corn free from any hard kernels; pour candy over it, mixing thoroughly. Spread lightly on a buttered marble slab or large platter, and when firm cut in pieces, or break up in little bunches of three to six kernels of corn.

Popcorn Cake

1 quart popped corn
1 cup sugar
¼ cup corn syrup
¼ cup water
2 tbsp molasses
1 tbsp butter
1 tsp salt

Pick over the popped corn, discarding all hard kernels, and finely chop the corn, or put through meat grinder, using a coarse knife. Put sugar, corn syrup, and water in saucepan, stir until it boils, and cook to 270°F (132.2°C), or until candy cracks when tried in cold water; add molasses and butter, and cook to 290°F (143.3°C), or until it is very hard when tried in cold water. Add corn, stir until well mixed, return to fire a moment to loosen it, then pour on buttered slab or tray, and roll with rolling pin as thin as possible. Cut in squares or break in small pieces. Molasses may be omitted.

Sugared Popcorn

2 quarts popped corn
2 tbsp butter
2 cups sugar
½ cup water

Pick over popped corn, discarding all hard kernels. Melt butter in saucepan, add sugar and water, stir until dissolved, and boil to 238°F (114.4°C), or until it will form a soft ball when tried in cold water. Pour over corn, and stir until every kernel is coated with sugar.

Brown Sugared Popcorn

Prepare as Sugared Pop Corn, using brown sugar instead of white.

Chocolate Sugared Popcorn

2 quarts popped corn
2 tbsp butter
2 cups brown sugar
½ cup water
2 squares chocolate

Pick over the corn, discarding all hard kernels. Melt butter in saucepan, add sugar, water, and chocolate. Stir over fire until chocolate is melted and boil to 238°F (114.4°C), or until it will form a soft ball when tried in cold water. Pour over corn, and stir until every kernel is coated with sugar.

Mock Violets

Popcorn
Fondant
Violet color paste
Angelica

Select large, open kernels of corn that will resemble the shape of violets. Color fondant a rich violet shade, melt it over hot water, and dip kernels of corn one at a time in the melted fondant, attach fine stems of angelica, place on paraffin paper, and leave until dry. Serve as a bonbon or use as a garnish on a bed of spun sugar around a mold of ice cream.

Popcorn Nests

Make popcorn balls and shape into hollow nests. Line with fringed wax paper, and fill with salted nuts or candies for a holiday dinner table.

CHAPTER XV

DECORATED Candies and Cakes

The appearance of many candies, as well as cake, is improved by flower decorations. Ornamental frosting, either cooked or uncooked, color pastes, a few sheets of stiff paper, and a pair of scissors, are all the outfit required. With a pastry bag and a tin rose tube, wedding and anniversary cakes may be decorated in conventional patterns with white frosting, and candies, like cream mints, can be shaped. Other decorations may be made with fondant, almond paste, and tiny candies. Practice is required to secure artistic results, but anyone with ordinary ability and patience can do excellent work. Pictures of cakes, or designs drawn on paper before putting on the decorations, will help to secure good results.

Holidays, birthdays, and other anniversaries may well be remembered with appropriate candies or cakes.

Uncooked Ornamental Frosting

2 egg whites
Sifted confectioners' sugar (icing sugar)
2 tsp lemon juice

Put eggs in a large bowl, add two tablespoons sugar, and beat 3 minutes, using a perforated wooden spoon. Repeat until one cup of sugar is used. Add lemon juice gradually, as mixture thickens. Continue adding sugar by spoonfuls, and beat until frosting is stiff enough to keep in shape after being forced through a pastry bag and tube. Color as desired.

With a pastry bag and variety of tin tubes, or with paper tubes, candies or cakes may be ornamented as desired.

Boiled Ornamental Frosting

1 cup sugar
1 cup water
¼ tsp cream of tartar
2 egg whites
Lemon juice

Put sugar and water in saucepan, stir until dissolved, bring to boiling point, wash down sides of saucepan with a piece of cheesecloth or a pastry brush dipped in cold water, add cream of tartar, cover, and boil 3 minutes, uncover, and let boil without stirring.

Beat whites of eggs in a large shallow pan with wire whisk until light but not stiff, and slowly add a spoonful of the boiling syrup, continuing the beating. Then add another spoonful of syrup in the same way, and a third spoonful. Continue beating the eggs until the boiling syrup spins a long thread, remove from fire, and add syrup in a fine steady stream to the egg mixture, beating constantly.

Set the dish containing the frosting in a dish of boiling water; the upper pan should fit tightly over the pan of hot water in order that steam may not escape. Gently fold the mixture over and over until it is stiff enough to hold its shape. Remove from the water, and very gently and slowly fold the frosting over and over until it is cool. Cover with a piece of damp cheesecloth. Frosting may be used at once, or will keep until the next day. With a variety of tubes and colors, beautiful and artistic decorations may be made on candies and cakes.

With a pastry bag and variety of tin tubes, or with paper tubes, candies or cakes may be ornamented as desired.

Paper Tubes for Decorating

A pastry bag of heavy drilling with a hole in the end through which can be inserted tin tubes with different kinds of openings, may be used for ornamental frosting, but sheets of linen foolscap paper, or strong thin typewriter paper, are quite as satisfactory. Cut the paper diagonally across, making two pieces measuring 8 x 11 x 14 inches. Shape the tube by taking one corner of the paper (1) in the right hand and the other corner (2) in the left hand, and rolling the paper around, making a cornucopia with a very sharp point at (3). The point of the funnel should be the center of the longest side. It may take some practice to learn how to hold and roll the paper, but it is really very easy to do when once understood. Turn in the edges of the paper at the open end of the cornucopia to hold it in shape, and cut an opening at the point.

For stems, dots, and writing, clip off the end of the paper funnel with a pair of scissors. For leaves, press the point of the funnel flat, clip off one fourth inch from the end, clip off corners, making another point, and make a slit one eighth inch long in each point. For some flower petals, clip off the point of the funnel, and cut the end in the shape of the letter W. For fine decorating, cut a small opening; for large full roses, or heavy flutings, cut a deeper slit. Have a paper tube for each color of frosting. With these tubes, almost any kind of ornamental frosting work may be done on candies or cakes.

How to Use Ornamental Frosting

Half fill a paper funnel with frosting, bring edges of open end together, and fold over twice, that frosting may not come out at the top. Hold the funnel in the right hand with the little finger toward the point of the tube and the thumb and forefinger closed tightly above the frosting. Force the frosting gently through the hole in the end of the tube by squeezing with the right hand and guiding with the left hand. Allow the tube point to rest lightly on the surface to be decorated. Conventional designs may be attempted at first, and soon it will be possible to make flowers and leaves. Colors should always be very delicate, and designs on candy should be small and dainty. Do not use a tube after it has become soft and out of shape at the point.

How to Color Frosting

Divide frosting into several portions, putting each portion on a saucer. Remove a bit of color paste from jar with a toothpick or steel skewer, and place on one side of saucer. Mix with a very small portion of frosting, then gently fold, not stir, into remaining frosting. Color each portion.

Forget-me-nots

Dilute a bit of blue or rose color paste with two or three drops of water or frosting, and gently fold it (do not beat it) into a small portion of ornamental frosting. In the same way color a small portion with leaf green, adding a tiny bit of blue if the color is not good. Color another portion with yellow. Make two stem tubes and one leaf tube of tough thin paper. Put blue or pink frosting into a stem tube, and force five tiny spots in a circle on the object to be decorated. Put green frosting into the two remaining tubes, and with the stem tube make a stem to the flower, and with the leaf tube, two forget-me-not leaves. Put a bit of yellow in the center of the flower with the point of a toothpick. It is well to have a blossom or a picture as a guide in making the design.

Wild Roses

Color portions of ornamental frosting rose and green. Put rose colored frosting in a leaf tube, and make four or five broad petals radiating from a center. Make stem and leaves with green frosting, and put a bit of yellow frosting in the center of the flower. For a double rose make a smaller group of petals inside the first group.

Large roses may be fashioned two inches in diameter, dried slowly in a cool oven, and used for decorating a dish of candies.

Sweet Peas

Color portions of ornamental frosting pink, red, lavender, and green, and put in leaf tubes.

Make one broad petal by forcing frosting through a leaf tube, then force two upright petals on center of first petal. The petals may be shaded by putting white frosting on each side of a tube and a colored frosting in the center, and forcing them out together. Add stem and leaves.

Violets

Color portions of ornamental frosting violet, green, and yellow. Make three broad violet or white petals that meet in the center, put a bit of yellow where they join, and add stems and leaves.

Lilies of the Valley

Color a portion of ornamental frosting green. Make with stem tubes a curved stem of green ornamental frosting, with five or six tiny blossoms of white frosting depending from it. Add one or two long narrow green leaves made with leaf tube.

Daffodil

With stem tubes make three tiny petals of yellow ornamental frosting, add a green stem, and two or three long slender leaves.

Decorated Peppermint Bars

Make After Dinner Mints, page 109, shaping the candy, when pulled, in bars four inches long and one inch wide. Let stand in confectioners' sugar until sugary, then decorate with a spray of roses or sweet peas made of ornamental frosting.

Decorated Mints

Make Plain White Mints, page 78, one and one half inches in diameter, and decorate with a single violet, forget-me-not, tiny rose, or holly berries and leaves made of ornamental frosting.

Decorated Marshmallows

Dip marshmallows in melted fondant, and decorate with tiny flowers made of ornamental frosting in different colors.

Edible Place Cards

Make Wintergreen Wafer mixture, page 145, roll thin, and cut in pieces two by three inches. Put ornamental frosting in stem tube, and write the name of each guest in the center of a card.

Marshmallow Baskets

Dip marshmallows in fondant, and when firm insert a piece of fine wire to make a handle. Fill stem tubes with ornamental frosting of different colors. Make a lattice work of frosting on the sides of the marshmallow, and cover the handle with frosting. Decorate with tiny stems and blossoms of contrasting colors, to make it look like a basket of flowers.

Orange Butter Frosting

⅓ cup butter
1 cup confectioners' sugar (icing sugar)
4 tbsp orange juice
1 tsp grated orange rind

Mix orange juice and rind, let stand half an hour, and strain through cheesecloth. Cream butter in a warm but not hot bowl. Add sugar gradually, and beat until light. Let orange juice get slightly warm, and add drop by drop to first mixture. This may be used for frosting candies or large or small cakes. Portions may be colored, and used through paper frosting bags for decorations. Keep in a cool place until needed.

Japanese Frosting

¼ cup butter
Sifted confectioners' sugar (icing sugar)
2 egg whites
Flavoring
Color paste

Cream butter, and add gradually half a cup of confectioners' sugar, beating constantly. Beat whites of eggs until stiff, and gradually beat in one cup of sugar. Combine mixtures, and add enough more sugar to make frosting stiff enough to hold its shape. Color and flavor as desired, and with paper tubes use to ornament candies or cakes. Keep in a cool place, that it may remain firm.

Christmas Tree Cake

Bake a cake two inches deep in a dripping pan. When cool, cut out in the shape of a Christmas tree on a standard.

Cover cake with Japanese Frosting, colored green, and flavored with orange flower water. Sprinkle with long shredded coconut colored green. Decorate the cake with tiny candies put on to imitate toys and candles. Place at the base toys fashioned from almond paste. Serve on a lace paper doily on a large plate or tray. Individual trees may be made if preferred.

Fondant or Almond Paste Flowers

Color fondant or almond paste to match the flowers that are to be made, using enough confectioners' sugar to make the mixture stiff enough to hold its shape. Model each petal separately, and fasten directly to the soft frosting of a cake, or complete the flowers and buds before frosting the cake. They may be kept several days before being used. Tiny birthday candles may be set in the center of each bud and flower if desired.

Leaves and stems may be cut from the green outside portion of a piece of citron and used to connect the flowers, making a graceful design on top and side of the cake. Poinsettias and holly at Christmas, roses, apple blossoms, orange blossoms, pansies, violets, and daffodils are all easily fashioned and most attractive.

Small flowers attached with a bit of frosting to plain mints are beautiful for afternoon teas, or to top a box of bonbons.

Caraway Decorations

Candied caraway seeds of different colors, and the very tiny candies known as 'hundreds and thousands', may be used to make most attractive decorations on candies or cakes. First make foundations of angelica. Cut angelica with a penknife into thin shavings, work with the hands into small balls, then flatten in lozenge shape, about three eighths inch in diameter. This makes a sticky surface. On it arrange a center of yellow or brown caraway candies broken in pieces, or use the 'hundreds and thousands', putting each candy in place with a small pair of tweezers, or the end of a toothpick dipped in water to make the candies stick to it. Around the center arrange white or yellow caraway candies like the petals of a daisy.

With the very tiny candies, a single yellow candy with five blue or pink candies around makes a forget-me-not. With yellow caraways, sprays of goldenrod or chrysanthemums may be fashioned. After the flowers are made, they may easily be arranged on the soft frosting of a cake, or fastened by means of sugar syrup to a large mint. Arrange leaves and stems to connect the flowers.

A basket may be made directly on the soft frosting of a cake in any color desired, having the candies go crosswise as a basket is woven. Leaves and stems may be made of fine strips of citron. The greenest citron that can be purchased and preferably the dark outside should be used.

Silver dragées may be used with the flower decoration for conventional designs.

Holly Decorations

Small red checkerberry candies may be purchased, the size and color of holly berries. Leaves may be fashioned from ornamental frosting, fondant, or almond paste colored green, or from angelica or citron. Halves of blanched pistachio nuts also make good leaves.

Arrange two or three leaves meeting at the center, place two or more red candies where they join, and a short stem of the same material as that used for the leaves. If the red candies are not obtainable, candied cherries may be cut the shape and size of holly berries, or fondant or almond paste may be colored with scarlet color paste, and shaped in small balls.

CHAPTER XVI

FAVORS

When children are being entertained, unusual sweets will always be appreciated, especially if there is something attractive to be carried home to be shown and later eaten. Decorated candies, described in the preceding chapter, will be found appropriate for this purpose, as well as the favors suggested in this chapter. Grown people are quite as pleased as children with something that represents individual and original effort.

Almond Fruits (Marzipans)

Work together equal parts by weight of almond paste and confectioners' sugar. Moisten with a mixture of equal parts of rose water and vanilla extract, and knead until well blended. Shape in a roll three fourths of an inch in diameter. Cut off pieces and shape with the hands to represent fruits or vegetables. Then color, using vegetable color paste diluted with water, applying it with a small brush. Tiny carrots, strawberries with green paper hulls, potatoes – the eyes made with a skewer, and the whole rolled in cinnamon – tiny pumpkins, walnuts, chestnuts, radishes, mushrooms, and many other shapes may be made with this mixture. The paste may be colored before modeling, and shaped into roses, daffodil, poinsettias, and other flowers, and used for decorating cakes and candies.

Chocolate Acorns

1 cup sugar
2 cups almonds
⅓ cup water
Chocolate shot or grated sweet chocolate

Put almonds in boiling water, and let boil gently 2 minutes; drain, plunge in cold water, again drain, rub off the skins, and dry between towels. Boil sugar and water to 290°F (143.3°C), or until it will crack when tied in cold water. Set saucepan in large pan of boiling water. Dip one end of almond into syrup, then dip into chocolate shot which will adhere to syrup on almond, and give it the appearance of an acorn in its cup. If syrup becomes too sugary while it is being used, add a little water, and bring to boiling point again.

Chocolate shot may be obtained at large grocery stores. It is composed of tiny pieces of sweet chocolate.

A Candy Bouquet

Gumdrops
Sugar syrup
Lace paper doily
Cardboard
Fine wire
Green tissue paper
Silver foil

This favor is to be in the shape of a small, old-fashioned bouquet. Make first a rule of gumdrops, coloring different portions of the mixture green, pink, red, yellow, or lavender. Shape the gumdrops in cornstarch like very small cones. Fasten a small lace paper doily to a three-inch disk of cardboard. To the back of the cardboard attach fine wires wound with green tissue paper and silver foil to imitate the stems. On the doily arrange leaves of green gumdrop mixture or mint jelly, and flowers of other colored gumdrops, fastening them in place with sugar syrup. Use as a favor at a luncheon or evening party.

Fig Favors

Figs
Raisins
Marshmallows
Almonds
Melted chocolate
Toothpicks or fine wire

With the above materials a great variety of attractive figures can be fashioned with a little ingenuity, and used as favors, or to hold a place card. Figs that come in bags, baskets, or glass jars should be provided, not the pressed figs. Almonds may be blanched, although it is not necessary. The materials are fastened together with toothpicks or wire, and are sometimes attached to cards, as a base, that they may stand upright.

An automobile can be fashioned with two or three figs for the body and back of the car, four marshmallows for wheels, a raisin on the end of a toothpick for steering wheel, and a man sitting in the car.

A man may be made with a fig for the body, raisins on toothpicks or wire for arms and legs, almonds for hands and feet, a marshmallow with features of melted chocolate for the head, and a fig with stem standing up on top for the cap.

An owl may have a body of one fig, head of another, bits of marshmallow for eyes and nose, and almonds for ears.

Popcorn Figures

Popped corn
½ cup sugar
¼ cup water
Melted chocolate
Chocolate peppermints
Chocolate creams
Marshmallows

Cook sugar and water until it cracks when tried in cold water. Dip kernels of popped corn, one at a time, in syrup, and put them together to make a body, arms, and legs of a boy or girl doll. Use a marshmallow for the head, putting on the features with melted chocolate. Attach a chocolate cream to a chocolate peppermint to make a hat, and fasten it to the figure with more syrup.

Different features and attitudes will give a great variety of members for the popcorn family.

Candy Dolls

Out of a double sheet of white tarlatan cut the figure of a boy or girl doll with a head a little larger than a large peppermint, and the rest of the body proportioned accordingly. Sew all the edges together except the head, which is left open until the bag is filled. Drop first into the bag tiny pink lozenges for toes and fingers, then large molasses peppermint balls for hands and feet. Use stick candy for arms and legs, fill the body with ribbon Christmas candy, use molasses peppermint balls for the neck, and for the head, a large flat round peppermint on which the features have been painted with color paste, and the hair and eyebrows with chocolate frosting.

Sew up the opening, and use for decoration on a Christmas tree.

Candy Animals

Cut figures of animals, such as elephants, dogs, or horses, from white tarlatan, leaving an opening on the back. Fill with candies, using sticks for legs and other candies for the bodies. Make eyes and ears as suggested for candy dolls, sew up the opening, and use on Christmas trees. Or use wintergreen wafer mixture or fondant, roll on marble slab, and cut out with animal shaped cutters. Paint on the features with melted chocolate.

Raisin Turtles

Select large plump raisins, insert a whole clove stuck through a currant for the head, four cloves for claws, and the small end of a clove for the tail. These may be used on top of a box of candy, or as a decoration for frosted cake or white mints.

Christmas Cards

1 tsp gelatine
2 tsp cold water
3 tsp boiling water
Few drops oil of wintergreen
1¼ cups confectioners' sugar (icing sugar)

Soak gelatine 5 minutes in cold water, dissolve in boiling water, and strain. Add flavoring and sifted confectioners' sugar, with enough more sugar to make stiff. Put mixture on board dredged with sifted confectioners' sugar, knead until perfectly smooth, then roll as thin as possible. Cut in circles two inches in diameter, or in pieces the size of visiting cards. To one small portion of trimmings add a bit of green coloring, knead, roll out, and cut or shape like small holly leaves. Color remaining trimmings bright red, and shape like holly berries.

Soak one teaspoon gelatine in two teaspoons cold water, and dissolve by standing over hot water. Brush under sides of leaves and berries with dissolved gelatine, and arrange on cards in an attractive design.

This mixture may be cut in any desired shape, and left undecorated if preferred.

Macaroon Baskets

Make macaroons (see page 164), having them less than one inch in diameter. Cook one cup sugar, half a cup of boiling water, and a few grains cream of tartar until syrup begins to discolor. Set saucepan in pan of cold water to instantly stop the boiling, then place in sauce-pan of hot water. Dip edges of macaroons in syrup, and place close together to form a circle large enough for the base of the basket. Around the edge fit a row of macaroons and over this a second row to make the sides of the basket, dipping the edges in syrup that they may stick together. When the basket is made, the syrup remaining in saucepan may be poured on a buttered tin, and kept in a warm place. As soon as candy can be handled, pull until glossy, and shape to form a handle for the basket. Dip the ends in melted syrup, and attach them to the sides of the basket. The baskets may be large or small, and used for ice cream or for holding candies.

Pecan Baskets

Follow recipe for Glacé Nuts, using pecans. As nuts are dipped, fasten two together for the bottom of the basket. Place others upright around the edge for the sides of the basket. Fashion handle as suggested in recipe for Macaroon Baskets, and fill with glacé strawberries.

Tables of Weights and Measures

Liquid Conversion Chart

Metric	Imperial	US
5 ml	¼ fl oz	1 teaspoon
15 ml	½ fl oz	1 tablespoon
30 ml	1 fl oz	⅛ cup
60 ml	2 fl oz	¼ cup
125 ml	4 fl oz	½ cup
150 ml	5 fl oz	2/3 cup
175 ml	6 fl oz	¾ cup
250 ml	8 fl oz	1 cup (1½ pint)
300 ml	10 fl oz (½ pint)	1¼ cups
375 ml	12 fl oz	1 ½ cups
500 ml	16 fl oz	2 cups (1 pint)
600 ml	20 fl oz (1 pint)	2½ cups

Weight Conversion Chart

Imperial/US	Metric
1 oz	25 g
2 oz	50 g
3.5 oz	100 g
4.5 oz	125 g
5 oz	150 g
8 oz	225 g
9 oz	250 g
16 oz (1lb)	450 g
35 oz	1 kg

Temperature conversion chart

Fahrenheit	Celsius	Gas mark
225°F	100°C	¼
250°F	125°C	½
300°F	150°C	2
325°F	160°C	3
325°F	170°C	3
350°F	180°C	4
375°F	190°C	5
400°F	200°C	6
425°F	210°C	7
425°F	220°C	7
450°F	230°C	8
500°F	250°C	9

Length Conversion

Inches	Centimeters
1.00"	2.54 cm
2.00"	5.08 cm
3.00"	7.62 cm
4.00"	10.16 cm
5.00"	12.70 cm
6.00"	15.24 cm
7.00"	17.78 cm
8.00"	20.32 cm
9.00"	22.86 cm
10.00"	25.40 cm
11.00"	27.94 cm
12.00"	30.48 cm

Approximate cup weight equivalents for some common dry ingredients

1 cup brown sugar	½ oz	210 g
1 cup chocolate, chopped	6 oz	150 g
1 cup cocoa	4 oz	110 g
1 cup coconut	2½ oz	80 g
1 cup confectioner's sugar (icing sugar)	4 oz	100 g
1 cup glacé cherries	6 ¾ oz	190 g
1 cup jam	12 oz	340 g
1 cup nuts, chopped	4 oz	110 g
1 cup plain flour	4 ½ oz	125 g
1 cup sultanas	5 oz	150 g
1 cup white granulated sugar	7 oz	200 g

Approximate cup weight equivalents for some common liquid ingredients

1 cup butter	8 oz	225 g
1 cup condensed milk	10.8	306 g
1 cup corn syrup	11 oz	328 g
1 cup cream	8 oz	225 g
1 cup honey	12 oz	340 g
1 cup maple syrup	12 oz	340 g
1 cup milk	8 oz	225 g
1 cup molasses	12 oz	340 g
1 cup oil	7.5 oz	210 g
1 cup sour cream	8 oz	225 g
1 cup vinegar	8.99 oz	255 g
1 cup water	8 oz	225 g
1 cup of yogurt	8 oz	225 g

INDEX

197

HESPERUS PRESS

Under our three imprints, Hesperus Press publishes over 300 books by many of the greatest figures in worldwide literary history, as well as contemporary and debut authors well worth discovering.

Hesperus Classics handpicks the best of worldwide and translated literature, introducing forgotten and neglected books to new generations.

Hesperus Nova showcases quality contemporary fiction and non-fiction designed to entertain and inspire.

Hesperus Minor rediscovers well-loved children's books from the past – these are books which will bring back fond memories for adults, which they will want to share with their children and loved ones.

To find out more visit www.hesperuspress.com
@HesperusPress